CRAZY HORSE

NORTH AMERICAN INDIANS OF ACHIEVEMENT

CRAZY HORSE

Sioux War Chief

▼ ▼ ▼

Peter Guttmacher

Senior Consulting Editor
W. David Baird
Howard A. White Professor of History
Pepperdine University

CHELSEA HOUSE PUBLISHERS

New York   Philadelphia

ACKNOWLEDGMENTS   The author gratefully acknowledges Mari Sandoz and Stephen A. Ambrose for the information, inspiration, and insights contained in their books. He also thanks Robin Brownstein for helping him in ways too numerous to mention.

FRONTISPIECE   This dress shirt, trimmed with hair from pony tails, resembles the costume Crazy Horse was given when he became a tribal leader. No photograph is known to exist of Crazy Horse or any of his possessions. When a white acquaintance asked him to pose for the camera, he apparently replied, "My friend, why should you wish to shorten my life by taking from me my shadow?"

ON THE COVER   Warrior, visionary, and Sioux patriot, Crazy Horse became known as one of the most powerful leaders in the fight for the northern plains.

Chelsea House Publishers
EDITORIAL DIRECTOR   Richard Rennert
EXECUTIVE MANAGING EDITOR   Karyn Gullen Browne
COPY CHIEF   Robin James
PICTURE EDITOR   Adrian G. Allen
ART DIRECTOR   Robert Mitchell
MANUFACTURING DIRECTOR   Gerald Levine

North American Indians of Achievement
SENIOR EDITOR   Marian W. Taylor

Staff for CRAZY HORSE
ASSISTANT EDITOR   Margaret Dornfeld
EDITORIAL ASSISTANT   Anne McDonnell
SENIOR DESIGNER   Rae Grant
PICTURE RESEARCHER   Lisa Kirchner
COVER ILLUSTRATOR   Michael Garland

Printed and bound in Mexico.

First Printing

1 3 5 7 9 8 6 4 2

Library of Congress Cataloging-in-Publication Data

Guttmacher, Peter.
Crazy Horse: Sioux war chief/Peter Guttmacher.
   p. cm.—(North American Indians of achievement)
Includes bibliographical references (p.   ) and index.
ISBN 0-7910-1712-5.
ISBN 0-7910-2045-2 (pbk.)
1. Crazy Horse, ca. 1842–1877—Juvenile literature. 2. Oglala Indians—Biography—Juvenile literature. 3. Dakota Indians—History—Juvenile literature. I. Title. II. Series.

E99.03C7234 1994   93-38545
978'.004975'0092—dc20   CIP
[B]   AC

CONTENTS

NORTH AMERICAN INDIANS OF ACHIEVEMENT

BLACK HAWK
Sac Rebel

JOSEPH BRANT
Mohawk Chief

BEN NIGHTHORSE CAMPBELL
Cheyenne Chief
and U.S. Senator

COCHISE
Apache Chief

CRAZY HORSE
Sioux War Chief

CHIEF GALL
Sioux War Chief

GERONIMO
Apache Warrior

HIAWATHA
Founder of the
Iroquois Confederacy

CHIEF JOSEPH
Nez Perce Leader

PETER MACDONALD
Former Chairman of
the Navajo Nation

WILMA MANKILLER
Principal Chief of the Cherokees

OSCEOLA
Seminole Rebel

QUANAH PARKER
Comanche Chief

KING PHILIP
Wampanoag Rebel

POCAHONTAS
Powhatan Peacemaker

PONTIAC
Ottawa Rebel

RED CLOUD
Sioux War Chief

WILL ROGERS
Cherokee Entertainer

SITTING BULL
Chief of the Sioux

TECUMSEH
Shawnee Rebel

JIM THORPE
Sac and Fox Athlete

SARAH WINNEMUCCA
Northern Paiute Writer and Diplomat

Other titles in preparation

ON INDIAN LEADERSHIP

by W. David Baird
Howard A. White Professor of History
Pepperdine University

Authoritative utterance is in thy mouth, perception is in thy heart, and thy tongue is the shrine of justice," the ancient Egyptians said of their king. From him, the Egyptians expected authority, discretion, and just behavior. Homer's *Iliad* suggests that the Greeks demanded somewhat different qualities from their leaders: justice and judgment, wisdom and counsel, shrewdness and cunning, valor and action. It is not surprising that different people living at different times should seek different qualities from the individuals they looked to for guidance. By and large, a people's requirements for leadership are determined by two factors: their culture and the unique circumstances of the time and place in which they live.

Before the late 15th century, when non-Indians first journeyed to what is now North America, most Indian tribes were not ruled by a single person. Instead, there were village chiefs, clan headmen, peace chiefs, war chiefs, and a host of other types of leaders, each with his or her own specific duties. These influential people not only decided political matters but also helped shape their tribe's social, cultural, and religious life. Usually, Indian leaders held their positions because they had won the respect of their peers. Indeed, if a leader's followers at any time decided that he or she was out of step with the will of the people, they felt free to look to someone else for advice and direction.

Thus, the greatest achievers in traditional Indian communities were men and women of extraordinary talent. They were not only skilled at navigating the deadly waters of tribal politics and cultural customs but also able to, directly or indirectly, make a positive and significant difference in the daily life of their followers.

From the beginning of their interaction with Native Americans, non-Indians failed to understand these features of Indian leadership. Early European explorers and settlers merely assumed that Indians had the same relationship with their leaders as non-Indians had with their kings and queens. European monarchs generally inherited their positions and ruled large nations however they chose, often with little regard for the desires or needs of their subjects. As a result, the settlers of Jamestown saw Pocahontas as a "princess" and Pilgrims dubbed Wampanoag leader Metacom "King Philip," envisioning them in roles very different from those in which their own people placed them.

As more and more non-Indians flocked to North America, the nature of Indian leadership gradually began to change. Influential Indians no longer had to take on the often considerable burden of pleasing only their own people; they also had to develop a strategy of dealing with the non-Indian newcomers. In a rapidly changing world, new types of Indian role models with new ideas and talents continually emerged. Some were warriors; others were peacemakers. Some held political positions within their tribes; others were writers, artists, religious prophets, or athletes. Although the demands of Indian leadership altered from generation to generation, several factors that determined which Indian people became prominent in the centuries after first contact remained the same.

Certain personal characteristics distinguished these Indians of achievement. They were intelligent, imaginative, practical, daring, shrewd, uncompromising, ruthless, and logical. They were constant in friendships, unrelenting in hatreds, affectionate with their relatives, and respectful to their God or gods. Of course, no single Native American leader embodied all these qualities, nor these qualities only. But it was these characteristics that allowed them to succeed.

The special skills and talents that certain Indians possessed also brought them to positions of importance. The life of Hiawatha, the legendary founder of the powerful Iroquois Confederacy, displays the value that oratorical ability had for many Indians in power.

The biography of Cochise, the 19th-century Apache chief, illustrates that leadership often required keen diplomatic skills not only in transactions among tribespeople but also in hardheaded negotiations with non-Indians. For others, such as Mohawk Joseph Brant and Navajo Peter MacDonald, a non-Indian education proved advantageous in their dealings with other peoples.

Sudden changes in circumstance were another crucial factor in determining who became influential in Indian communities. King Philip in the 1670s and Geronimo in the 1880s both came to power when their people were searching for someone to lead them into battle against white frontiersmen who had forced upon them a long series of indignities. Seeing the rising discontent of Indians of many tribes in the 1810s, Tecumseh and his brother, the Shawnee prophet Tenskwatawa, proclaimed a message of cultural revitalization that appealed to thousands. Other Indian achievers recognized cooperation with non-Indians as the most advantageous path during their lifetime. Sarah Winnemucca in the late 19th century bridged the gap of understanding between her people and their non-Indian neighbors through the publication of her autobiography *Life Among the Piutes*. Olympian Jim Thorpe in the early 20th century championed the assimilationist policies of the U.S. government and, with his own successes, demonstrated the accomplishments Indians could make in the non-Indian world. And Wilma Mankiller, principal chief of the Cherokees, continues to fight successfully for the rights of her people through the courts and through negotiation with federal officials.

Leadership among Native Americans, just as among all other peoples, can be understood only in the context of culture and history. But the centuries that Indians have had to cope with invasions of foreigners in their homelands have brought unique hardships and obstacles to the Native American individuals who most influenced and inspired others. Despite these challenges, there has never been a lack of Indian men and women equal to these tasks. With such strong leaders, it is no wonder that Native Americans remain such a vital part of this nation's cultural landscape.

1

CRYING FOR A VISION

High on a lonely butte in the Sand Hills of present-day Nebraska, a slender, light-haired boy called Curly lay staring at the sky. For three days he had been away from his home and family, fasting and praying. To keep himself from sleeping, he had jammed stones between his toes and spread pebbles on the ground beneath his back. Exposing his body to the sun and wind, shivering to the sound of the wolf's howl, the 13-year-old Oglala boy had given himself to Wakan' Tanka, the Great Spirit. He was now weak with hunger and exhaustion and hoarse from prayer, and still he had received no answer.

Curly was desperate. He had seen the whites—with their wagon trains, their whiskey, and their cannons— erupt in a storm of violence. He had seen his tribesmen, driven by anger and fear, strike out at people they had once tolerated in peace. The dark confusion he had witnessed in the past few days had left a powerful chief mortally wounded and turned the Brulé and Oglala Sioux into fugitives in their own country. Curly was so disturbed by the turmoil that had suddenly entered the lives of his people that he was seeking the aid of the spirits early, before reaching the age of 15, when Sioux custom allowed a boy to leave his home for several days to fast and pray and wait for a vision, a sign that would tell him about

An 1837 painting by Alfred Jacob Miller shows Sioux warriors surveying the Platte River at a popular crossing place. From the early 19th century on, the Sioux and other plains Indians hunted, camped, and communicated with white traders in this region.

11

his future. Ignoring tradition, Curly had neither discussed the matter with his elders nor gone through the usual preparations, purifying his body with a sweat bath and the smoke of sweet grass and sage. With the sound of gunfire still ringing in his ears, he had left his family even as they fled the scene of the conflict, hoping a waking dream would offer him counsel.

Curly's people were the Hunkpatila band of the Oglalas, a powerful branch of the great Sioux Nation. The Sioux had gone through many changes over the past century, but now, in the 1850s, they were the strongest and most united population on the northern plains. Their seven western council fires—the Oglala, Brulé, Minneconjou, Hunkpapa, No Bow, Two Kettle, and Blackfeet tribes—controlled a vast region stretching west from the Missouri River to the Bighorn Mountains and north from the Platte River to the Black Hills. In hunting, horsemanship, and war, the Sioux's skills were unsurpassed.

Yet even during their rise to prominence, white traders had been putting down roots within Sioux territory, and the U.S. Army had been sending out troops to protect the American citizens who settled on Indian soil. Over the past few decades, trading posts had sprung up, first along the Missouri, then on the North Platte River, and large groups of Indians had begun to frequent these posts, exchanging animal skins for metal goods, firearms, food, and alcohol. Though most Indians appreciated the value of the manufactured goods that could be purchased at the forts, some of them worried about the changes the whites seemed to be bringing to their people. They saw the apathy, recklessness, and belligerence that took hold of men and women who grew drunk on whiskey, and they watched disapprovingly as groups of Indians set up permanent camps around the white outposts and traded their old ways for alcohol and other ready-made supplies.

Emigrants travel west on the Oregon Trail in a romantic landscape by Albert Bierstadt. An Indian village can be seen in the distant background.

Calling their more susceptible tribesmen Loafers-about-the-Fort, many Sioux bands—Curly's people among them—made a point of avoiding the posts when they were not directly involved in trading.

Meanwhile, other whites had been blazing a trail across Sioux territory, preparing the way for settlers headed for the fertile country of the Far West. At first only small groups of travelers ventured forth along the Oregon Trail, as the road came to be called, and the Indians watched them pass with little more than curiosity. As the stream of settlers swelled, however, their curiosity changed to uneasiness, then to a resentment that eventually flared into hostility.

Little by little, the emigrants' livestock grazed and trampled wide tracks of grassland down to dirt; their axes damaged the cottonwoods that dotted the plains; their gunfire decimated the buffalo herds and frightened smaller game away. Trudging across the plains in an endless chain of covered wagons, the whites brought with them such diseases as measles, smallpox, and cholera— foreign ailments for which the Indians had no immunities and no cure. Most of the settlers held the Indians in contempt and pushed their way through Sioux territory as if it were their own.

The Indians began to see the destruction of their hunting grounds and the epidemics that ravaged their villages as part of a plot to drive them from their country. They took revenge in the form of small-scale raids, demanding tribute from the travelers, stealing their property, and in general building up a steady pattern of harassment. Finally the U.S. government, responding to settlers' demands for protection, set up a post at the biggest trading town on the North Platte River and manned it with a small detachment of soldiers.

In 1851, the government made a more concerted effort to halt the warfare on the plains, calling Indian leaders from all across the region to a council at Horse Creek near Fort Laramie, as the new post on the North Platte was called. There, U.S. agents drew up a treaty requiring the Indians to give safe passage to whites who traveled the Oregon Trail. In return, the government promised to give the Sioux annuities—yearly supplies of such goods as guns, ammunition, flour, sugar, coffee, tobacco, blankets, and bacon—for 55 years. After weeks of turbulent discussion, most of the Indians, lured by the prospect of regular gifts from the government, agreed to the terms of the treaty. They also agreed to recognize a chief from the Brulé tribe, Conquering Bear, as the leader and spokesman of all the Sioux, although the idea of a head chief was alien to them.

Despite the agreement, friction between Indians and whites continued. Along the Holy Road, as the Sioux now referred to the emigrant trail, the Indians continued to badger the travelers. Sometimes a few of them would approach the covered wagons to trade or extract gifts of food or other small items. A more defiant warrior might steal into an emigrant camp at night and make away with a metal pot, knife, or rifle. On occasion, a brazen Sioux would sweep in by daylight and cut out horses and cattle from the travelers' herds.

Meanwhile, more Indians moved their camps to the region around Fort Laramie and let their lives drift

Fort Laramie, pictured here, had been a trade center for the Sioux for many years before the U.S. government bought it from the American Fur Company. After the Treaty of 1851, in which the government promised the Indians a yearly supply of goods, a number of Sioux bands made the area near the post their permanent home.

toward dependency. Even those who scorned the "trader" life and continued to travel and hunt in the traditional way came to the fort each summer to receive their share of the annuity.

And so it happened that in the summer of 1854, after the Sun Dance and the buffalo hunt, Curly's band joined other Oglalas and Brulés and, under the leadership of the Oglala chief Man Afraid of His Horse, moved to a spot a few miles south of Fort Laramie, not far from the emigrant trail. That summer, as in years before, the government agent was long in coming. The Indians passed the time trading their buffalo robes for coffee, whiskey, and other goods at the posts of Jim Bordeaux—a white who had married into the Brulé tribe—and the American Fur Company. Young warriors pestered the emigrants on the Holy Road according to their usual custom, more for sport than for profit.

Then, on August 17, an incident occurred that was to shatter Indian-white relations all along the Platte River. Among the emigrants traveling the Oregon Trail that day was a party of Mormons, and as they passed the Sioux settlements, one of their cows wandered into a Brulé camp. The owner went to retrieve the cow, but when he saw the large gathering of Indians, he became frightened and retreated. Whether out of spite, boredom, or simply habit, a visiting Minneconjou warrior sank an arrow into the animal, and the Indians butchered and ate it. To the Sioux, this act was no different from any of the other exploits that typified life along the Holy Road, and they gave it little thought.

The men at Fort Laramie felt differently. Life at the army outpost—a tiny island of white influence in the vast wilderness of Indian territory—had proven tedious and unproductive, and the men who served there were souring. The Indians had become a constant problem, begging, thieving, and frightening the emigrants in the very face of U.S. forces. For years the Indians' mobility, endurance, and knowledge of the land had made them almost impossible to restrain, let alone punish. Frustrated at their own ineffectuality, some of the soldiers had begun to lead random attacks on Sioux warriors they found riding alone. Career advancement on the frontier was usually grindingly slow, and the more ambitious soldiers knew that an impressive performance on the battlefield could speed the process. Most of the men at Fort Laramie were eager to prove themselves in combat; for them, a raiding Minneconjou was excuse enough for war.

The day after the cow was killed, its owner went to the post's commanding officer, Lieutenant Hugh B. Fleming, and demanded action. At least one senior officer, Lieutenant John L. Grattan, was elated. Isolation and inactivity had already driven the 24-year-old West Point graduate to drunken bragging; with only 20 soldiers and a cannon, he said, he could whip the whole Sioux Nation. Now, declaring that he "hoped to God there would be a fight," Grattan urged Fleming to avenge the Mormon, who said he meant to "have them injuns cleaned out like a nest of snakes."

Fleming summoned Conquering Bear to the fort. The chief agreed to pay the Mormon $25, although the frail old cow was probably worth about half that amount. The offer was not enough; Fleming told Conquering Bear that the offender, High Forehead, would have to come in to face justice. The chief, who did not regard the Minneconjous as subject to his control, objected, suggesting instead that the Mormon come to his personal herd of ponies and take the best in place of the cow. But Fleming ignored this offer too, announcing that his men would be paying the Brulés a visit the following day. On his way back to the Brulés, Conquering Bear passed through the

George Catlin, an ethnographer and artist who spent many years documenting Native American tribes, painted this portrait of an Oglala warrior in 1832. Over the Indian's left shoulder is draped a buffalo robe, one of the staples of Sioux trade.

Oglala camp and told the Indians there what had happened. Unsure what the soldiers had in store for them, the men at both camps began to prepare for war.

On August 19, 1854, Brulé and Oglala scouts watched the tiny line of 31 blue-coated soldiers wind its way downriver toward the circle of lodges that made up the Brulé camp. The Indians had gathered their weapons and corralled their pony herds; the women and children had slipped back into the willows along the river's edge. One band of warriors waited at the camp, armed and painted; other Indians hid along the rise behind the encampment and up on the surrounding ridges. Curly, although barely 13, was allowed to stay with the older men to witness the parley.

The army unit, wielding a 12-pound cannon and a mountain howitzer, paused at the outskirts of the Brulé camp. Leading the troops was Grattan, accompanied by his mixed-blood interpreter, Auguste Lucien. As Grattan rode up to meet Conquering Bear, Lucien, no friend to the Sioux, raced his pony back and forth in front of the tense encampment, as a warrior would before battle. Half-drunk and beside himself with excitement, he threatened the Sioux, saying he would carve them a new set of ears so they could hear the whites' words better and swearing he would eat their hearts for breakfast.

Conquering Bear, still hoping to avoid a confrontation, approached Grattan with the ceremonial peace pipe; the lieutenant ordered his troops to load their cannons. The chief deposited five marked sticks before Grattan, each representing a man of standing who was willing to give the Mormon the choicest pony from his herd. Grattan ignored him, demanding that he produce the Minneconjou. Finally, the chief agreed to speak to High Forehead, but after a brief absence he returned to say that the warrior, who lurked among the painted Brulés, refused to give himself up. While Curly and his tribesmen looked on in suspense, negotiations continued for nearly half an hour. Then, suddenly, whether in response to a misunderstanding—caused, perhaps, by Lucien's defects as an interpreter—or through sheer impatience, Grattan ordered his men to open fire.

The warriors watched in horror as Conquering Bear dropped to the ground, nine bullets in his body. The next instant they attacked, pouring out of the camp and down from the bluffs, descending on the white men from all sides. High Forehead brought Grattan down with a single bow-shot; the rest of the soldiers fell in a matter of minutes. Lucien fled and hid in an empty lodge; Sioux warriors dragged him out, killed him, and mutilated his body. Their anger unappeased, the Indians stormed over to Jim Bordeaux's, where the trader heaped them with supplies in an attempt to calm them. Finally, fearing retaliation, they packed their belongings, lifted their wounded chief onto a travois, and fled to the east.

Curly had gone with the Brulés, his mother's people, who were carrying Conquering Bear. Disturbed by the recent bloodshed, the chaotic flight, and the thought of the dying chief, he had gone out on his own to seek peace with himself at an isolated spot on the wide prairie. Now, lying parched and aching on the hillside, Curly was able to think about all he had seen and heard. He knew the Sioux had taken a dangerous step and that everything had changed.

To do his part in this difficult time, Curly needed to be shown what path he should take in life. He could be a warrior, a hunter, or a holy man. He could be a man of peace like Man Afraid of His Horse, who had struggled to keep the younger men from burning down the soldiers' fort before leaving. He might even become the great leader that his father hoped for, one who would turn back the whites and return the plains to the Sioux. Pale, serious, and reserved, Curly sensed that he was different from other boys, and he may have hoped to learn that he, among all his people, had a special role to play. But three days had passed, and he had learned nothing. Dejected, he finally gave up, struggled to his feet, and walked unsteadily toward the spot where he had hobbled his pony. After several steps he fell unconscious.

A lake shimmered before him. From its depths a

warrior surfaced, riding intently forward on a horse that looked like his own, but floated, danced, and constantly changed colors. Bullets and arrows flew around them, yet the strange warrior and his horse remained unharmed. The warrior was dressed in plain blue leggings and a buckskin shirt. His face was unpainted, and he wore his long brown hair unbraided, adorned only with a single feather. He had a small brown stone tied behind his ear, but he carried no scalps or war trophies.

Suddenly a storm churned up behind the vision rider, forcing him on into the shower of lead and arrows, and a crowd of people—his own people—swarmed around him, trying to grasp his arms and hold him back. Still mounted on the floating horse, he broke their grip and seemed to become part of the storm itself. A lightning bolt struck down his cheek, and white spots, like hail, appeared all over his body. A red-tailed hawk screamed overhead, and everything faded into blackness.

Curly awoke to find his father and his closest friend, Hump, standing over him. They were relieved to see him alive, but they were also angry; he had ridden off alone, without warning, into territory regularly visited by their enemies, and it was a tense, troubled time for everyone. Curly was silent. He did not speak of the vision and would not for almost three years, although he knew that his cry for guidance had been answered. He may have sensed that the vision he had seen was one of deep power, and even that his life would be marked by enormous strength and courage. Yet as he stumbled down from the hilltop alongside his father, he may have also felt that in many ways, he was not yet ready for his calling. He would have to grow, learn, and prove himself to his people many times over before he could begin to serve them as the great Sioux leader, Crazy Horse.

2

ᐁ ᐁ ᐁ

CURLY

In the fall of 1841, at a place called Bear Butte, just northeast of the Black Hills of present-day South Dakota, an unusual boy was born into the Hunkpatila band of the Oglala Sioux. Small and pale, with a narrow face, he resembled neither his father, an Oglala holy man named Crazy Horse, nor his mother, a sister of the prominent Brulé warrior Spotted Tail. As the boy grew older, his light brown hair grew out in soft waves, and he was given nicknames to match: Light-haired Boy, Curly Hair, or, most often, Curly.

Curly probably spent his first months the way most Sioux children did, rubbed down with buffalo fat for warmth and protection from dryness and infection, diapered with absorbent moss, and tucked securely into a cradleboard on his mother's back, ready to travel with his people. If he cried too loudly, his mother may have quieted him with a quick pinch of his nostrils; the Hunkpatilas often moved through enemy territory, and lessons in silence could never begin too early. His mother and other women in the band nursed him, and as he grew bigger and stronger, they began to feed him bits of chewed buffalo dipped in soup. The adults around him all had a hand in his upbringing; their lodges were open to him, and Curly, like other children, could enter any

An Oglala chief, wearing ceremonial feathers and paint, poses for a portrait by George Catlin. The painting was completed just a few years before Crazy Horse was born.

23

of them when he was in need of food, drink, or affection. When he was old enough to talk, he addressed not only his parents but also his aunts and uncles as mother and father, and all the older people in the band, regardless of their relation, were "grandparents."

Little is known of Curly's early childhood, but he probably grew up in an atmosphere of great warmth and tenderness. He had an older sister who helped care for him, and before long he also had a younger brother. His father was a well-respected member of the tribe who came from a family known for humility and good will. Sioux men and women loved to play with their children, and they rarely punished them, encouraging them instead to move around freely, to follow their own impulses and explore the world in whatever way they pleased.

Their world was wide, for the Hunkpatilas, like other Sioux Indians, were almost constantly on the move. In the spring, they might shift locations as often as twice a week to allow their pony herds to keep grazing on the prairie's new grasses. They continued to move periodically throughout the summer, following the buffalo herds, raiding the camps of their Pawnee, Omaha, and Shoshone enemies, and visiting the area around Fort Laramie to trade away their buffalo robes and dance and feast with the other Indians congregated there.

At each new stopping place, the children made fresh discoveries, and their energy and curiosity helped to keep the Indian encampments lively. The American historian Francis Parkman spent a summer with the Hunkpatilas in 1846, when Curly was five years old. At the time, Curly's village spread across several acres just south of the Platte River near the Oregon Trail, and Parkman remembered it as bursting with activity:

> Warriors, women, and children swarmed like bees. Hundreds of dogs, of all sizes and colors, ran restlessly about;

and close at hand, the wide shallow stream was alive with boys, girls, and young squaws, splashing, screaming, and laughing in the water.

Curly would have spent some of his summer days helping his mother harvest plums, turnips, currants, buffalo peas, onions, and fox grapes. Toward the end of the season, he may have joined other children pounding dried choke-cherries into dried buffalo meat and kidney fat to make *wasna*, the preparation that nourished his people on the trail and through the winter. Little by little, with the help of older members of the tribe, he learned to read the signs his people lived by: a flying swallow with a muddy beak was coming from a watering place; wild

In this painting by Worthington Whittredge, a group of Indians crosses the North Platte River toward a shaded encampment. The Oglala Sioux might camp at such a site for several days, then move on to fresh hunting grounds.

horses walking in a string were usually going toward water.

Children also took part in games and contests, often wagering toys or other small possessions on the results. They might play catch, using balls of hide stuffed with antelope hair, or practice tossing arrows through a willow hoop. They engaged in pony races, swimming competitions, and wrestling matches; they formed teams and pelted each other with mud. In time, the girls dropped out of these games and turned to playing with dolls, taking care of younger children, and learning to do household tasks. They tended to keep to themselves, and the boys for the most part left them to their own activities, but when everyone came together around the campfire at night, it was not unusual for the bolder boys to tease them, pitching plum pits at them across the smoke.

Most of the games Sioux children played helped prepare them for adult life. As they grew older Curly and his friends, emulating the tribe's warriors, would hunt squirrels with small bows and arrows. They also played "Buffalo Hunt," shooting arrows at a hole carved in a cactus that one of the boys carried on a raised stick. The one who shot through the target—the buffalo's heart— got the privilege of taking up a cactus paddle and pricking the carrier's behind. Boys might compete with each other in acts of daring, seeing who could pilfer a piece of meat from a drying rack without getting caught or ramming their ponies together and trying to knock each other to the ground.

As they struggled to outdo their peers, Sioux boys remained keenly aware that one of the highest qualities a Sioux warrior could possess was the ability to withstand pain without flinching. They learned this from the stories their elders told of great warriors and their bravery in battle, from the boasting they heard from the men returned from war, and from tribal ceremonies celebrating courage and stoicism.

The most sacred and spectacular ceremony practiced by the Sioux was the Sun Dance, performed during the summer in the country around the Black Hills. During this ritual, men and women pledged their devotion to Wakan' Tanka, the Great Spirit, who provided them with buffalo and supported them in battle. Worshipers usually danced for days without food or water, exposed themselves to the elements, and stared into the sun for long periods of time. The dance often ended only when the participants passed out from exhaustion. To express their devotion, many Indians—usually men—committed painful acts of personal sacrifice. Some would cut small patches of skin from along their arms and legs and continue to dance while bleeding. In a more elaborate ritual, worshipers fastened heavy buffalo skulls to the flesh on their backs and danced until the skulls ripped free. In another, warriors pierced their pectoral muscles, ran lengths of rawhide from their chests to the tip of a sapling, then strained against their tethers until the leather tore through their skin. Those who took part in the Sun Dance often received visions in the course of their ordeals; depending on the extent of their suffering, they could also win considerable prestige.

Throughout this time of worship, children enjoyed as much freedom as they did the rest of the year and in fact were given special license to harass their elders. They could poke shirtless men with spears of sharp grass, surprise them with ashwood popguns, and sneak into their tents with a sharp tool and puncture their water bags, all without fear of reprimand. Black Elk, a Sioux holy man who grew up during the 1870s and whose memories were recorded by the novelist John G. Neihardt, said of his early days at the Sun Dance, "We were allowed to do almost anything to tease the people, and they had to stand it . . . for everybody was supposed to endure everything." Most children—boys especially—looked forward to the time when they too would be able to perform the Sun Dance, communing with the Great Spirit and exhibiting their own strength and perseverance.

Winter came early to Sioux territory, and the change of season brought an end to dancing, raiding, hunting, and feasting. By late October, most villages were moving from their prairie encampments to the sheltered canyons of the north, where they would wait out the blizzards and the days of bitter cold. Winter was a time for stories to be told and traditions to be passed down. Gathered around the warm fire, children learned about their people's past, about medicinal plants and how to use them, about weather patterns, and about animals—their secrets, their strengths and weaknesses, and their multifaceted relationship with the Sioux. The young Sioux would store up this knowledge and wait for the day when spring would again arrive and they could test what they had learned on the open prairie.

To be part of this nomadic life, Curly had to learn how to swim and ride at an early age. He learned to navigate broad expanses of territory, to find food when game was scarce, and to recognize friends and enemies. By the time he was in his early teens, he would be joining the older men on pony raids, war missions, and hunting expeditions.

In August 1851, when Curly was about 10 years old, his band attended the Fort Laramie Treaty Council at Horse Creek in present-day Wyoming. At the council were some 10,000 Indians, representing all the major tribes of the plains. Hoping to win their favor, the government agents who had called the meeting showered the Indians with gifts, and for nearly a month, the Indians feasted lavishly as they discussed the terms of the treaty. One missionary who witnessed the festivities was offended by the Indians' taste for dogmeat: "No epoch in Indian annals," he said, "probably shows a greater massacre of the canine race."

The government's proposals were far-reaching. Officials at the council were asking the Indians to allow white settlers to cross their lands; they were dividing the plains into separate territories and asking each tribe not to cross the borders of its own district or wage war on any other tribe; they were asking every Indian nation to select a leader who could speak for everyone. Many Indians objected to the treaty, and it was only after weeks of negotiations that a sizable group of leaders—a group that did not include the Oglalas—agreed to sign.

After the council, the members of Curly's band went back to their usual routine, roaming the lands to the north of the Platte River, far from Fort Laramie and its stultifying influences, often traveling with their close allies, the Brulés. At about this time, Curly found a companion in a young Minneconjou named Hump. A skilled warrior and a frequent guest of the Oglalas, Hump agreed to take the boy under his wing and serve as his *kola*, or mentor. Hump made the boy his first bow and war club and rode, hunted, and scouted with him for days at a time.

The following year, Curly joined a group of boys tracking a herd of wild horses in the Sand Hills, the area where he would later receive his vision. Curly proved his boldness by capturing and breaking a horse before any of the others. In honor of his achievement, his father gave him a new name, His Horse Looking. Though the name was rarely used, the young Sioux probably understood that he had taken his first step toward manhood.

Horsemanship played a pivotal role in the life of a

warrior, and the skill of Sioux riders was legendary. Their preferred breed, the pinto ponies that ran wild on the plains, were smaller than the emigrants' horses, but for endurance, it was said, they could not be matched. Sioux riders, likewise, had the strength to cover enormous distances; they could hunt, fight, and even sleep on horseback. Before he had reached his early teens, Curly was learning how to come to the aid of a warrior who had lost his horse in battle, sweeping by him at a full gallop and lifting him up onto his own pony. He may also have learned to perform one of the most impressive feats of Native American combat: riding slung so far over his horse's side that he could shoot a bow accurately from under its neck.

When Curly returned to camp with his newly captured pony, he would have been following Sioux custom if he

A herd of wild horses stampedes across the prairie in this painting by Alfred Jacob Miller. The artist, who came across the herd on an 1837 expedition to the West, wrote in admiration: "They wheel like trained columns of cavalry, charge, scatter, and form again . . . stopping for a moment,—snuffing the breeze, . . . and are gone."

had boasted loudly of his accomplishments. Sioux warriors, the pride of their community, were expected to sing their own praises, coming home from the hunt and the battlefield with proud stories of the dangers they had faced and the valor they had shown. A warrior's bragging helped the tribe celebrate his victories, and most boys caught on to this tradition early, exaggerating every act of courage they could claim as they moved toward adulthood.

Men and boys who wished to be considered successful might also try to enhance their image by wearing elaborate clothing, jewelry, or emblems of their achievements. A warrior might set out for battle in a buckskin shirt covered with intricate beadwork, his braids wrapped tightly in strips of weasel or beaver fur, his arms circled with bands of hammered silver, and his hair adorned with notched and painted feathers that pictured his many exploits. As soon as they could acquire such finery, most Sioux boys would parade their wealth in the same way.

Curly, however, was different from other boys. He avoided displays of pride, wealth, or emotion. He dressed plainly, spoke little, and tended to retain a quiet, controlled exterior. Curly's reserve expressed itself not only in his attitude toward his accomplishments, but also in his response to tribal events. During periods of mourning, when most of his people would signal their grief by tearing their clothes and cutting their skin or their hair, Curly did not participate. When the tribe danced—even when they performed the Sun Dance—he preferred to stay on the sidelines. According to the men and women who knew him, Curly was a very private boy who seldom revealed his thoughts, but who took in all that was happening around him.

In the fall of 1854, some time after the conflict at Fort Laramie and the troubled days in which Curly received

This George Catlin sketch shows Sioux women dressing buffalo hides outside their tipis. The woman on the left has hung a cradle board from the poles of a stretching rack so that she can watch her infant as she works.

his vision, the boy returned from a hunting trip with the news that he had killed his first buffalo. He had been out with Hump in the region northwest of Laramie, where game was scarce from frequent hunting. After two days without results, Curly put his ear to the ground and heard the faint rumble of a buffalo herd a full two days' ride away. On hearing the news, the Oglala band sent scouts ahead to track the animals while the warriors mustered a hunting party. Curly joined the hunt and, to his parents' pride, managed to kill two buffalo: a yearling and a two-year-old.

For the Sioux, as for many other tribes, buffalo was a sacred animal; it was also a good provider. Buffalo meat, considered superior to beef by many visitors to the plains, could be roasted, dried, or boiled into soup, with a pinch of gunpowder for seasoning. The liver, a coveted delicacy, usually went to the hunter immediately after the kill. Once the Sioux had butchered a buffalo, they found all kinds of uses for the parts that remained. A warrior might whittle a buffalo-bone needle, thread it with sinew, and sew a water bag from the buffalo bladder. Buffalo leg bones became scrapers, knives, and awls. The Indians made ribs and jawbones into children's sleds and boiled buffalo hooves for glue. Hides made clothing, blankets, drums, lassos, and bridles; 16 to 20 of them sewn together could make a tipi, the portable, cone-shaped tent that Sioux families called home.

The night after Curly's successful hunt, his band butchered the kill, and as drying racks groaned under their load of meat, the Indians held a great celebration. While Hump danced through the Oglala camp, singing Curly's praises, Curly himself hung back in the shadows. Whether or not he wished to claim his glory, the boy had clearly distinguished himself as a hunter; it would not be long before he made his mark as a warrior as well.

That fall, while the Oglalas were hunting to the north, a band of Brulés—still embittered over the loss of their chief—had been hovering near the Holy Road, raiding the whites in defiance of the Treaty of 1851. In November 1854, Curly's uncle Spotted Tail led four Brulé warriors in an attack on a mail coach heading east toward Fort Laramie along the Oregon Trail. The Brulés killed both the driver and the man seated next to him, put an arrow in the leg of an escaping passenger, and found themselves in possession of $20,000. What happened to the money is not certain, but they probably spent it at Jim Bordeaux's trading post. The Brulé raids continued into the spring. The pickings were easy, and there was no need to depend on annuities from a tardy Indian agent.

While most of the Oglalas were camped well to the

north of Fort Laramie at this time, many of the tribe's more ambitious warriors drifted south to take part in the action, and Curly was among them. In the summer of 1855, Curly accompanied his uncle and a band of warriors on a pony raid southeast of the Platte River. One part of the band soon split off and headed for the Loup River and the villages of the Pawnees. Curly's group, meanwhile, waited for nightfall, then crept into an Omaha camp, cut loose the horses they found hobbled there, and drove them north. By daybreak the Omahas were on their trail, and not long afterward, they engaged the Brulés in combat.

In the course of the skirmish, Curly, not yet 15, spotted an Omaha crawling through the brush. He lifted his bow and arrow and fired. Approaching the body, he discovered that he had killed a woman, not a warrior, and was momentarily taken aback. In the Sioux tradition, it was no dishonor to kill an enemy woman; the Sioux believed that warriors would fight twice as fiercely to protect their women in battle and that any man who could thwart them was merely demonstrating his own superior strength and skill. Still, something inside the young warrior would not let him take the woman's scalp; empty-handed, he rejoined his companions.

The Brulé band came away from the fight victorious; they had killed three Omaha warriors, lost none of their own, and acquired a handsome new herd of ponies. Some of the Indians may have thought it strange that Curly forfeited an enemy scalp; years later, those who spoke of him remembered a little song his people had made up to tease him: "A brave young man comes here, but a foolish one without a good knife!"

Meanwhile, the Grattan Massacre, as the whites had dubbed the conflict at Fort Laramie, had not been forgotten. Newspapers in the East were buzzing with stories of the Sioux vandals and the carnage they had left behind them, and outraged citizens clamored for revenge. In the summer of 1855, while Curly was learning the rudiments of combat, General W. S. Harney, a hero of the Mexican War, was assembling a force of 600 men at Fort Leavenworth, Kansas. His troops were to move up the Oregon Trail to Fort Laramie, then sweep northeast through some 250 miles of Sioux country toward Fort Pierre, in the center of what is now South Dakota. Their mission was to punish the Sioux.

3

STRONG MEDICINE

In August 1855, the Indian agent at Fort Laramie sent runners to all of the Sioux tribes, ordering the Indians to move south of the Platte River. Those who did not, he warned, would face the wrath of the U.S. Army. More than half of the Sioux bands, a large number of Oglalas among them, obeyed the agent, and by September as many as 400 Sioux lodges were clustered around Fort Laramie. Almost all of the Minneconjous and most of the Brulés, however, ignored the order and continued to hunt and camp as they saw fit.

By this time Spotted Tail and his followers, including Curly, had joined forces with the Brulé leader Little Thunder and were camped with his band on Blue Water Creek, just north of the Platte. When the agent's messengers arrived with the order to move, Little Thunder assured his people that they would be safe where they were. How he came to this conclusion has never been clear, but he posted no scouts and left his village defenseless, in a valley surrounded by wooded hills. He had as few as 100 warriors with him and a much larger number of women and children who needed protection. At dawn on September 3, 1855, while Curly was away hunting, General Harney—his infantry, cavalry, and artillery in tow—arrived outside of Little Thunder's

The Oglala chief Bull Bear poses in traditional buckskin dress, holding an ax of white manufacture. The leader was killed during a feud between two Oglala factions whose quarrel flared under the influence of alcohol.

37

General William S. Harney, a veteran Indian fighter, led a punitive campaign against the Sioux in the summer of 1855. Although known for his severity on the battlefield, he was a firm believer in the power of negotiation.

camp. Having sent his mounted men up into the hills to circle behind the sleeping village, Harney led the rest of the troops directly into the valley. The sound of the marching soldiers woke Little Thunder and Spotted Tail, and the leaders, shocked at the sight of Harney's regiment, rushed out with a white flag to parley. Little Thunder started talking, perhaps hoping to give the women and children time to pack up and escape. Harney was happy to comply; he was letting his cavalry move into position.

When the cavalry was ready, the talking stopped, and Harney chased the Brulé leaders back into the camp.

Little Thunder urged his people to retreat, and they did—right into the onrushing cavalry. Within 30 minutes, nearly 100 Indians—mostly women and children—lay slaughtered, and some 70 more had been taken prisoner. Little Thunder, Spotted Tail, and most of the other survivors scattered onto the open prairie.

As Curly approached the valley that night, he saw smoke rising from the spot where the village had been. Advancing cautiously, he soon came upon a horrifying scene: dozens of men and women, their scalps removed, lay sprawled among the charred remains of the Brulé homes. As Curly walked further, his attention was drawn by a faint moaning. He followed the sound and, lifting a pile of buffalo robes, discovered a Cheyenne woman, clutching her dead infant and weaping over the loss of her husband. Curly recognized the survivor as Yellow Woman, a guest of the Brulés. He found a travois to carry her, and together they left the valley, hoping to overtake Spotted Tail and the rest of the survivors. Later Yellow Woman, the niece of a powerful Cheyenne medicine man, would praise Curly ardently for this kindness; the incident began a lifetime bond between the young warrior and her people.

Harney, meanwhile, was marching his captives in chains to Fort Laramie. At the fort he had them imprisoned and told the agent he was neither to release them nor to distribute any annuities until the Indians who had attacked the mail coach, together with the $20,000 they had stolen, were turned over to the military. Within two weeks of Harney's order, Spotted Tail, who had fought valiantly at Little Thunder's camp and fled with four bullet wounds in his body, resolved to turn himself in. With so many of his people—his small daughter among them—imprisoned and at the white man's mercy, he may have felt he had no choice. Still,

The Brulé leader Spotted Tail became an advocate of peace after two years in captivity at Fort Leaven-worth, Kansas. In this 1877 portrait he is shown wearing white-style clothing.

the decision required great courage; according to Brulé accounts, he believed he was going to his death. Outside Fort Laramie, dozens of Sioux idlers watched in suspense as the six-foot chief and a loyal warrior, Iron Shell, approached their fate. In the end, Harney spared the Indians' lives, put them in chains, and sent them to prison at Fort Leavenworth, Kansas. Chastened and subdued, Spotted Tail would come back two years later, an advocate of peace and cooperation with the powerful whites.

Hoping to impress the Indians further, Harney continued his march to Fort Pierre; he did not encounter a single Sioux, so deeply had his act of terror affected them. The general's style of warfare—the "rub out," as the soldiers called it—was new to the Sioux. Most plains Indians went to war not so much to defeat an enemy as to demonstrate their own courage, and their battles rarely produced more than a few casualties. Warriors did bring bows and arrows, and sometimes guns, to battle, but they saw little honor in using these weapons. As they saw it, striking an enemy from a distance did not require much courage; a far braver thing was to kill by the knife or war club. Indians could gain just as much prestige by "counting coup"—getting close enough to an opponent to touch him with a lance, a coup stick (a tool made especially for this purpose), or, better yet, a bare hand. Taking an enemy's weapon from him, rescuing a friend who had lost his horse, even receiving a frontal wound in combat brought a Sioux warrior higher honors than did destroying an enemy army. One missionary who lived with the Santees, an eastern branch of the Sioux, from 1835 to 1845 carefully documented their nearly constant combat with four other tribes. During the 10 years he knew the band, he noted only 88 Sioux casualties and 129 enemy losses. In their encounter with Harney, then, the Sioux had essentially suffered a decade's worth of fatalities; there is little wonder that his "rub out" left them reeling.

From Fort Pierre, Harney sent word to the Sioux chiefs that they were to meet him in council the following March. Most of them agreed to come, and that spring the chiefs signed a new treaty, promising once again to stay away from the emigrants on the Holy Road. Without consulting the Sioux, Harney also appointed Bear Ribs, a Hunkpapa leader, to the position of head chief in the place of Conquering Bear. At one point in the meeting, the general tried to impress on the chiefs the extent of the whites' power through a show of "magic" involving the recently developed anesthetic, chloroform. "Why, we can kill a man and then restore him to life," he reportedly told the Indians. To demonstrate, Harney ordered his surgeon to render an Indian dog unconscious, then passed the dog around for inspection. When the chiefs were convinced that the dog was dead, the surgeon applied the restorative. Despite his efforts, the dog did not revive, and the Indians only laughed, remarking that the white man's medicine was too strong.

Harney did not know it, but by the end of the March council, the Sioux had made plans to hold their own meeting the following summer. They would gather north of the Black Hills at Bear Butte and decide on a unified policy for dealing with whites.

Before the Bear Butte council was held, Curly spent several months drifting between the Brulé and Oglala camps, training for his future as a hunter and warrior. Early in the summer of 1857, he accompanied Man Afraid's son, known as Young Man Afraid of His Horse, and a group of Oglalas on a visit to a Cheyenne village on the Solomon River in Kansas. There he witnessed further bloodshed. The Cheyennes, whose territorial rights were also being challenged by the U.S. Army, had decided to try using medicine to stop the white man's bullets. A holy man named Ice, the same man whose niece Curly had rescued two years earlier, had the warriors of his band dip their hands in a small lake while he chanted over them, declaring that the treatment would shield them from injury in battle. On July 29, the Cheyennes rode open-palmed against a six-company cavalry led by Colonel E. V. Sumner, believing they could catch bullets in their bare hands. Confused, the soldiers never fired, but they drew their sabers and cut into the Indians as they fled. At the end of the rout, four Cheyennes lay dead.

Shaken by this catastrophe, Curly—still only 15 years old—must have been happy to leave Cheyenne country and arrive safely at Bear Butte, where he was reunited with his family and his mentor, Hump. The boy soon learned that his brother, three years his junior, had already shown so much daring in war parties against the Crows that he had inherited his uncle's name, Little Hawk.

Camped in a huge circle of tipis, as many as 7,500 Sioux assembled at Bear Butte that August. The council gave Curly a chance to meet many celebrated warriors from other tribes: the Hunkpapa chief Four Horns and his nephew, Sitting Bull; Long Mandan of the Two Kettles Sioux; Crow Feather of the No Bows; and Lone Horn, a Minneconjou chief, along with his seven-foot-tall son, Touch the Clouds.

The Sioux found inspiration in the large number attending the Great Teton Council, and as they discussed their troubles they made many vows of resistance. Yet no further decisions came out of the council. The Indians chose no leader, they established no network of communication, and they made no provisions for the main task ahead of them: fighting opponents who outgunned them by a ratio of nearly 100 to 1.

The tribes scattered after the council. Man Afraid's Oglalas rode for the western edge of the Black Hills to hunt buffalo, and Curly's family traveled with them for a while. At some point along the way, Curly and his father separated from the group and rode off alone. Curly was almost a full-grown warrior now, and it was time for him to reflect on the responsibilities he would face as an adult. He and his father made a sweat lodge, smoked, and fasted. It was at this time that Curly finally told his father of the vision he had seen during the flight from the battle at Fort Laramie. Crazy Horse, impressed with what he heard, interpreted the dream, explaining to his son that the phantom warrior was the man he was to become. If Curly followed the example of the dream rider, if he dressed as he did and acted as he did, never taking scalps or other prizes for himself, he would never be struck by enemy arrows or bullets. Crazy Horse believed that his son had been given a powerful medicine, and he asked him to use it wisely, leading his people bravely, helping the weak, and providing for the hungry.

Curly may have realized that to follow this path would take much courage and sacrifice. His vision was there to guide him, however, and as he faced his awesome destiny as leader of the Sioux, the memory of the spirit rider would continue to serve as his anchor and inspiration.

That fall, Curly and his father joined a group of Oglalas

This painting shows a peaceful gorge in the Black Hills, a favorite winter hunting ground of the Sioux. By the late 1850s, the Oglalas and other northern bands had entered a new region northwest of the hills, near the Powder River in northern Wyoming and Montana.

and Minneconjous hunting buffalo near the western edge of the Black Hills. By this time, the traditional hunting ground of the northern Sioux, just north of the Platte, was nearly depleted. Between the emigrants traveling the Oregon Trail and the Indians living around Fort Laramie, the buffalo herds that had once darkened that part of the plains had shrunk so drastically that the Sioux could no longer survive there. Keenly aware of this, Curly's Oglalas and the other independent bands were gradually moving into an area that was new to them: the prairies northwest of the Black Hills, close to the Powder River. They would have to fight for this land, which was now in the hands of the Crows, the Arapahos, and the Shoshones.

By the summer of 1858, Curly was ready to prove himself in battle. He had prepared himself in the manner of his vision. His father had made him a medicine bundle of sacred objects to take with him into combat; it included a powder made of dried eagle brain and aster flowers, which he was to chew and rub over his body. A red-backed-hawk feather adorned his loose hair, and a small brown stone had been tied behind his ear. He had painted a lightning bolt of red earth from his forehead to the base of his chin and white hail spots on his body. He was ready to try to become what he had dreamed.

Curly's first campaign was to take him farther west than the Oglalas had ever traveled, to the Wind River country of what is now central Wyoming. The Indians who lived in that region, the Arapahos, were said to be peaceful and in possession of a fine herd of ponies.

As it turned out, the Arapahos—hardly the docile victims the Oglalas had hoped for—were ready and waiting. They had gotten wind of the raid, and by the time the Sioux reached their village, they had positioned themselves on top of a hill. Before moving in to attack, the Sioux circled the rise slung to one side of their horses

so they were shielded from enemy fire, trying to goad their opponents into wasting lead and powder, but the trick failed. The Arapahos kept their weapons carefully aimed at the few warriors who attempted to crawl up toward them. The fight proceeded. Guns blasted, arrows whizzed, and for all their tactics the Oglalas were kept at bay.

The contest had been going on for about two hours with little progress on either side when suddenly Curly's horse was shot out from under him. The Oglalas, already preparing to retreat, probably expected the young warrior to run and take cover, but Curly's vision instructed him otherwise. Suddenly, before his companions' unbelieving eyes, he caught hold of a loose pony and charged uphill through a hail of arrows and bullets. He reached the top untouched, drove a lethal arrow into an Arapaho warrior,

Indians camp near the Wind River in this 1865 painting by Alfred Jacob Miller. It was in this region that Curly—soon to be called Crazy Horse— first made his mark as an intrepid warrior.

then whirled to race back down, his tribesmen whooping in admiration.

Before Hump could offer him praise, Curly turned and charged through another barrage of arrows and lead, killing a second warrior with a blast from his pistol. Then, seeking a token of his bravery, he slipped off the pony to lift the scalps of the men he had killed. No sooner did he have his trophies in hand than an arrow struck his leg and the horse bolted from his side. Forced to run for his life, he found shelter behind a rock, where Hump removed the iron arrowhead and tied a strip of fresh horse skin around the wound. Taking the scalps had been a mistake. After this day, with one exception, he would never again ignore the message of his guiding vision.

The Oglalas carried on with the attack until the battle was declared successful, then turned toward home, sending a man ahead to announce their victory. They had killed four enemy warriors, counted many coups, taken some good horses, and lost not a single man. Curly's courageous charge had turned the tide of the battle. Still, when the victory dance was held, he refused to tell of his accomplishments.

Late the next morning, as Curly slept and healed, his father strode through the village, singing a song of praise:

My son has been against the people of unknown tongue.
He has done a brave thing; for this I give him a new
name, the name of his father, and of many fathers before
him. I give him a great name. I call him Crazy Horse.

4

▼ ▼ ▼

THE MAKING OF A
WARRIOR LEGEND

A Sioux warrior, wearing a large feather headdress, ornamented leggings, and a buffalo robe, poses for an 1839 portrait by Charles Bodmer.

The early 1860s were good years for the northern Oglalas. After their successful raid against the Arapahos, Man Afraid's warriors were able to drive the Crows and Shoshones from large expanses of land around the Powder River and take control of a region where buffalo and other game were plentiful. With the Civil War raging, the whites were too involved in their own troubles to bother harassing Indians in the West, and for the most part the Sioux felt free to hunt and raid as they had in the past.

Crazy Horse continued to prevail in battle, often riding and fighting at Little Hawk's side. Both warriors fought fiercely, but Crazy Horse, as he gradually discovered, had a further asset: a mind for strategy. His friend He Dog would later comment: "[Crazy Horse] didn't like to start a battle unless he had it all planned out in his head and he knew he was going to win. He always used judgment and played safe."

Crazy Horse fought with a cool head, and his people learned to admire him for it. They also began to see that his quiet, serious temperament—the modesty that made him so different from other Sioux warriors—was part of what made him successful. More interested in the future of his people than in personal glory, Crazy Horse had a reputation for keeping Sioux casualties down and seeing to the safety of the wounded. His bravery and skill were never questioned, and as he amazed his people again and again with uncanny feats of daring, he offered still further proof of the power of his medicine: after his mishap at the Wind River, he was never again struck by an enemy in battle.

In June 1861, during a raid on a Shoshone hunting party near the Sweetwater River, the young warrior's medicine was severely tested. Just as the Oglalas were making their escape, Crazy Horse's mount was shot from under him, and before he could rescue his brother, Little Hawk suffered the same mishap. As the Shoshones advanced around them, the brothers, cut off from their fellow warriors, found themselves firing back fallen arrows as fast as they could for lack of ammunition. The circle tightened, but for awhile the brothers, shooting frantically, managed to keep their assailants from charging.

Finally, during a brief lull, two Shoshone warriors rushed forward to cut the brothers down in hand-to-hand combat. According to the Oglala warrior Short Bull, who told the story to an interviewer years later, Crazy Horse shouted to Little Hawk, "Take care of yourself—I'll do the fancy stunt!" He gave a quick lunge to the right, and his attacker followed, allowing Crazy Horse to twist around and grab the Shoshone's leg, yank him to the ground, and mount his horse. He turned to find that Little Hawk had shot his own attacker and taken his horse, and the two raced off to the east, laughing.

As his fighting style matured, Crazy Horse made his

medicine even stronger by adding a talisman made for him by a childhood friend, an Oglala medicine man called Chips. The charm was a small, white stone, threaded onto a buckskin string that he wore slung over his shoulder so that the stone rested under his left arm, protecting his heart.

Before long, Crazy Horse and his astonishing fighting power acquired the stature of myth. Sioux warriors, firmly convinced of his invulnerability, followed him with confidence into battle. The Crows, who later called Crazy Horse the most fearless Sioux they ever fought, would tell of a magic rifle he had that hit whatever he looked at. Desperate for a way to defeat him, they eventually traveled as far as Nez Perce country, in western Idaho, in order to buy a special medicine that, it was said, would at least bring death to his horses.

A Crow warrior pursues a pair of Sioux Indians in a drawing completed by a Crow chief in 1884. During the 1860s, Crazy Horse and other Sioux led countless raids against the Crows and their allies, the Shoshones.

As a successful warrior, Crazy Horse gained early entrance into the Crow Owners society, one of the men's organizations, called *akicitas*, that ensured order in Sioux villages. The main role of the akicita was to make and enforce tribal law. Sioux chiefs, though deeply respected, did not have the power to tell tribe members what to do or to punish them for bad behavior. The Sioux followed a chief only as long as they felt he was worthy, and they remained free to leave any chief's band whenever they chose. While they were a part of a band, however, they were governed by that group's akicita, whose members had enough authority to stop a fight, destroy the tipi of a thief, or banish a murderer. An akicita's most important day-to-day task was to keep order during hunts and war parties, operations in which ambitious young warriors, left to their own devices, might jeopardize the success of the group for their own personal glory.

Crazy Horse must have seemed the perfect akicita member: fearless, selfless, and self-disciplined, he commanded universal respect. As a Crow Owner, he had the right to join other members of the society at the frequent private gatherings where they talked, smoked, and laughed together for hours at a time, but he rarely made use of this privilege.

Around 1860, when Crazy Horse was 18 years old, he began to court Black Buffalo Woman, a niece of Red Cloud, the renowned leader of the Bad Face Oglalas, a group that had split off from the Hunkpatilas some years before. Sioux custom allowed unmarried men and women to meet in the presence of their elders. If they wished, they could stand close to one another with a blanket wrapped around them to achieve a measure of privacy while they talked. Not all young people followed these rules, but Crazy Horse, as his friend He Dog would later comment, "was a very quiet man except when there was

An unmarried Sioux woman poses for a portrait by George Catlin, who described her as "much esteemed by the whole tribe, for her modesty, as well as beauty." When Crazy Horse was about 18, he courted Black Buffalo Woman, a young Oglala whose charms were also widely admired.

fighting," and he probably acted according to the wishes of the young woman's parents.

Unfortunately, Crazy Horse was not the only candidate for the hand of Black Buffalo Woman. Crazy Horse continued to live modestly, refusing to flaunt his success and giving away the horses he claimed in battle. Meanwhile, another warrior, No Water, was busy gathering a large pony herd that he hoped would honor the woman's parents and impress her respected uncle. In the spring of 1862, Red Cloud organized a war party against the Crows, and both Crazy Horse and No Water helped to lead it. A short way from the Bad Face village, No Water developed a severe toothache and returned to camp. When Crazy

Horse came back with the party two weeks later, he was greeted by his impudent friend Woman's Dress, who announced that someone had been "walking under the blanket" with Black Buffalo Woman in his absence. No Water and Black Buffalo Woman had married.

Mortified, Crazy Horse retreated to his mother's tipi, and after two or three days of solitude during which he refused to eat or speak, he bolted off to fight the Crows once more. Weeks later, he returned with the last scalps he would ever take, fed them to his dogs, and began making a sweat lodge to purge his embittered soul.

Crazy Horse had suffered a personal setback, but on the battlefield, he and the rest of the Oglalas continued to prosper. Even as their influence spread, however, they

Gold miners take a break from their work digging, washing, and filtering gravel along the banks of a creek in 1852. Eventually, rumors of gold sent thousands of prospectors like these into the heart of Sioux territory.

began to notice new signs of white activity, this time near their hunting grounds and sacred lands in the Black Hills. Back in 1857, the Indians had encountered a topographical survey team traveling to the Black Hills—and trespassing on lands the Sioux had been guaranteed in the Treaty of 1851. The Sioux had driven this group away, but the following year a military party had explored the area and returned to the East with the news that they had found gold. With the discovery of more gold in western Montana a few years later, white prospectors began clamoring for safe passage from the Oregon Trail to the center of Sioux territory.

In 1863, frontiersman John Bozeman arrived in Montana Territory and marked a path running southeast from the Yellowstone River to the North Platte, right through the heart of Sioux hunting grounds. When Bozeman entered their territory again, this time with a larger crew and a wagon train of supplies, a party of Oglala, Minneconjou, and Cheyenne warriors assembled and surrounded the travelers 150 miles into their northward journey and, after a week-long siege, succeeded in driving them away.

That same year, the Santee Sioux—a tribe that had continued to live in present-day Minnesota, where settlers had flooded their lands and driven them to extreme poverty—staged a bloody uprising. After killing 100 whites in a battle at the town of New Ulm, the Santees ravaged settlements all across their former country, spreading terror throughout the upper Mississippi valley. The whites' revenge was terrible. The U.S. Army not only devastated large Santee villages but pursued the survivors west, attacking nearly every Indian who crossed their path. Soon the Indians of the southern plains retaliated by raiding the Oregon Trail with renewed ferocity, burning wagon trains, ranches, and transport stations, and perpetuating the turmoil.

In August 1864, the governor of Colorado issued a proclamation urging citizens to form bands and hunt down any "hostiles" in their vicinity. Colonel John M. Chivington, the military commander in Denver, promptly amassed a rabble of more than 600 90-day volunteers and set out to attack a Cheyenne band camping at Sand Creek, about 40 miles north of Fort Lyon in southeastern Colorado.

The leader at Sand Creek, Black Kettle, had long been at peace with the whites. He had been promised safety by the Fort Lyon commandant and even flew an American flag in the center of his village. As Chivington's forces entered his camp at dawn on November 29, 1864, Black Kettle continued to assure his people that they had nothing to fear. After the soldiers fired their first volley, Black Kettle raised a white flag of truce. The firing continued.

On December 26, 1862, the U.S. Army executed 38 Santee Sioux to punish the tribe for an uprising against Minnesota settlers. This lithograph documents the event.

When Chivington was asked whether to spare the tribe's women and children, he is said to have replied, "Kill and scalp all, big and small, nits make lice!" More than 150 Cheyennes lost their lives that morning. Among the casualties was Yellow Woman, the Cheyenne whom Crazy Horse had befriended after the massacre at Blue Water Creek.

The survivors of the Sand Creek massacre fled north to the Powder River country. Meeting with their Indian allies—the northern Cheyennes, the Sioux, and the Arapahos—they told them of their grief, then passed a pipe among them. Whoever smoked it pledged himself to war. In December, some 6,000 Indians gathered at the headwaters of the Smoky Hill River, below the North Platte in eastern Colorado. The band included such illustrious Sioux leaders as Red Cloud and Sitting Bull, as well as the famed Cheyenne chief Roman Nose. The

Colorado militia under Colonel John M. Chivington surround Black Kettle's village at Sand Creek. Below the American flag in the center of the Cheyenne camp waves the Indians' white flag of truce.

northern Oglalas sent only a few warriors, but Crazy Horse was among them.

On January 7, 1865, the Indians made their first raid, hitting a stagecoach station in Julesberg, southeast of Laramie in Colorado Territory. After chasing the troops at nearby Camp Rankin into their stockade, the Indians set about plundering the Julesberg station, store, and company warehouse, then launched further attacks on the surrounding ranches and wagon trains. George Bent, the half-Cheyenne son of a trader in the region, recalled watching the Indians pack up huge amounts of flour, cornmeal, rice, sugar, molasses, coffee, ham, bacon, canned goods, dried fruit, and clothing and load them onto their ponies. The raiders had no idea what many of the items were for, and they asked Bent to explain. When told that ketchup, dried fruit, and imported cheeses were special delicacies, one group combined the three for a feast and ended up violently ill.

The raiding continued for almost a month. Crazy Horse rode with his friend Little Big Man, joining the many Sioux, Cheyenne, and Arapaho warriors as they scoured the entire valley south of the Platte. Bonfires blazed every night as the Indians came together in a massive encampment to celebrate their success. Captain Eugene F. Ware, one of the soldiers trapped at the Camp Rankin stockade, later wrote of the experience:

> We could hear them shrieking and yelling, we could hear the tum-tum of a native drum, and we could hear a chorus of shouting. Then we could see them circling around the fire, then separately stamping the ground and making gestures. . . . We knew that the bottled liquors destined for Denver were beginning to get in their work and a perfect orgy was ensuing. It kept up constantly. It seemed as if exhausted Indians fell back and let fresh ones take hold.

On February 2, 1865, the band packed up and headed north for the Powder River country. Men, women, and

A band of plains Indians performs a torchlight scalp dance. In January 1865, Cheyennes, Sioux, and Arapahos could be heard reveling in their triumphs during an extended campaign against white settlements south of the Platte River.

children trekked some 400 miles through the bitter cold, stealing property and livestock, tearing down telegraph wires, and destroying a large section of the Overland Stage Line along the way.

News of the Indian victory put fire in the hearts of the northern Oglalas. In May, Young Man Afraid of His Horse and Red Cloud came together to plan a second attack on the Platte region that summer. Leaving their ponies to graze and gain strength, Young Man Afraid and Crazy Horse led a band of warriors south for some preliminary raids. Not long after their campaign began, a crisis hit the Sioux who lived near Fort Laramie. The Civil War was now over, and a new set of officers had been sent west to put the plains in order. General G. M. Dodge, the new commanding officer of the region, soon learned that there were Indians living right outside Fort Laramie. Unable to grasp the reasons for their presence, he banished them all to Fort Kearney, Nebraska. On June 11, 1865, under the guard of 135 soldiers, more than 1,500 Sioux—Indians who had long ago ceased to hunt, wage war, or make a living from the land—started out for their new home, 300 miles to the southeast, in the heart of Pawnee territory.

Hearing of this disaster, the raiding Oglalas sent a party of warriors to the area to rescue the captives. On the night of June 13, Crazy Horse slipped into the camp of the exiled Sioux, distributed weapons among them, and informed their headmen that a large party of Oglalas waited for them to the north, across the North Platte.

When the Indians were slow to start the next morning, an army captain rode into their camp with a few of his men to investigate. Behind the dust kicked up by the soldiers' horses, many of the women slipped away and forded the river, which had been marked with sticks for easy crossing. The remaining men, their weapons concealed, caused as much commotion as possible during the ensuing head count. Finally, the captain bellowed a few insults, and a warrior abruptly shot him. As the remaining soldiers fled to seek reinforcements, the Indians raced for the river. Almost all the Sioux managed to escape, and the troops, infuriated, burned the encampment.

As the rescued Indians scattered northward, the Oglalas

headed back toward the Powder River, where a joyful reception awaited them. They had resolved to fight the whites, and their successes had been spectacular. Still, the war was far from over; more soldiers were on their way, and their sights were set on Powder River.

5

RED CLOUD'S WAR

Celebrating the Sun Dance during the summer of 1865, the Sioux gave thanks to the Great Spirit for their recent victories and asked to be strengthened for the battle ahead of them. Together with their allies, they were coordinating an ambitious two-pronged attack on white centers of transport and communication. To the north, Sitting Bull and his Hunkpapas agreed to strike Fort Rice on the Missouri River in present-day North Dakota. Further south, some 1,000 lodges of Sioux, Cheyennes, and Arapahos were to unite and attack the army at the bridge that brought the Oregon Trail across the North Platte River slightly northwest of Laramie.

Crazy Horse, following his usual custom, did not take part in the Sun Dance. Instead, when the ceremony had ended, he spent several weeks drilling his warriors and meditating on the medicine of his vision. He was 24 years old and in excellent fighting condition, though he may have weighed no more than 140 pounds. Going into battle, he had continued to dress sparely, never wearing more than a breechcloth and plain leggings in anything but the coldest weather. Meanwhile, his brown hair had grown long enough to hang down past his waist when not braided, and his personal rituals had grown more complex. Before fighting, Crazy Horse would take dirt

The Oglala leader Red Cloud would eventually become one of the most powerful men in the Sioux Nation. In 1866 he summoned warriors from all over the northern plains to help his people drive the whites from the Powder River region.

and spread it over himself and his horse, moving his hand in a particular pattern, the meaning of which was known only to him. Sometimes he took the stone that he wore to protect his heart and rubbed it over his body as well. His friend Chips had made him an eagle-bone war whistle, which he wore on a thong around his neck, and he had acquired another sacred stone to tie to his horse's tail. Crazy Horse had other quirks as well: when the ceremonial pipe was passed around before a battle or discussion, he would refuse to smoke unless each smoker had tamped the tobacco down with his thumb.

In late July, the great war party of Sioux, Cheyennes, and Arapahos set off for the south in full battle regalia, with Roman Nose, Young Man Afraid, and Red Cloud in the lead. After a three-day march they set up their village just south of the Platte Bridge near Fort Casper. Their plan was to draw the troops out with a decoy, then overwhelm them on the open field, where their fighting power was strongest.

On July 25, 1865, Crazy Horse and a band of about 20 warriors approached the bridge from the north. They gestured toward the army's pony herd on the other side and unfurled their blankets as if preparing to wave them at the horses and start a stampede. Soon a company of troops was rushing across the bridge with a howitzer in tow. The soldiers stopped at the north end of the bridge, and the decoys simulated panic, pretending to whip their ponies, trying to entice the soldiers to follow them over the next ridge, where as many as 3,000 Indians were waiting to engulf them. When the soldiers did not take the bait, Crazy Horse and his companions fired a few antagonizing shots at their reluctant pursuers, who returned their fire with a few rounds from the howitzer. Apparently, the sound of gunfire was too much for the impatient warriors waiting on the other side of the ridge.

First two or three of them, then the entire Indian force broke away and charged up the hill to see what the noise was about. The troops took one look at the sea of galloping warriors and thundered back to safety.

Crazy Horse may have realized that an Indian tradition—the tendency to sacrifice all in the name of personal bravery—had botched the initial strike. For the next few days, he and his band repeated their attempt to lure the soldiers out of the fort, but without success. According to some accounts, the operation eventually degenerated to the point where the decoys forgot the plan and really did go after the army's horses. Finally the party gave up and began to drift back north. Though the ratio of Indians to whites had easily been 100 to 1, by the end of their campaign they had managed to kill only eight soldiers, and the bridge that had been their target remained intact. The Oglalas later learned that Sitting Bull had experienced the same frustrations at Fort Rice.

That fall, in response to their organizational problems, the northern Oglalas revived a governing system that had been out of use since the first days of the Holy Road. Three Oglala villages came together to discuss the matter. They decided to follow the old tradition and select seven "Big Bellies"—respected leaders who had reached the age of 40—whose role would be to advise and govern the people. Four younger warriors, meanwhile, would be chosen to serve as "Shirt Wearers," enforcing the laws made by the Big Bellies and taking responsibility for the tribe's day-to-day decisions. These new leaders would work together to create order and unity in the entire tribe.

The Big Bellies, chosen by general agreement, took office soon after the decision was made. For the selection of the Shirt Wearers the Indians put together a great ceremony. Their camp, situated at the time about 70 miles northwest of Fort Laramie, consisted of a huge circle of tipis with an enormous council lodge in the center. A trader and interpreter named Billy Garnett was there and later described the scene. At the start of the festivities, the sides of the council lodge were rolled up to permit everyone to see, as the Big Bellies waited and smoked inside. A group of opulently dressed horsemen then set out from the center and rode around the circle of tipis four times, each time drawing a warrior from the crowd and leading him into the council lodge. Young Man Afraid, Sword, and American Horse, all sons of Big Bellies, were the first three to come to the center. The fourth Shirt Wearer came from a family that was neither rich nor prominent. As the ceremonial horsemen made their final circuit, they passed by a number of warriors who were both able and well connected, then wound their way to the back of the crowd and summoned a man whose skill and courage in battle outweighed his humble origins: Crazy Horse. The Sioux greeted all four selections with loud trills of approval.

Once inside the council lodge, after much feasting the young men received their sacred shirts. Each was sewn from the skins of two bighorn sheep, the forelegs making the sleeves and the hind legs hanging in back. Quill work across the shoulders depicted objects that were sacred to each wearer. The sleeves were fringed with locks of hair, each lock representing a brave deed, a coup, or a sacrifice made on behalf of the Sioux. Crazy Horse's shirt is said to have contained more than 240 such locks.

When a single feather had been fastened flat against the back of each man's head, an older member of the tribe, one familiar with the Shirt Wearer tradition, rose and said to them:

> Wear the shirts, my sons, and be big-hearted men, always helping others, never thinking of yourselves. Look out for the poor, the widows and orphans and all those of little

power; help them. Think no ill of others, nor see the ill they do to you. . . . Do not give way to anger, even if relatives lie in blood before you. I know these things are hard to do, my sons, but we have chosen you as great-hearted. Do all these duties gladly and with a good face. Be generous and strong and brave in them, and if for all these things an enemy comes against you, go boldly forward, for it is better to lie a naked warrior in death than to be wrapped up well with a heart of water inside.

The elder's words were well timed; even as the Oglalas celebrated the return of the Shirt Wearer tradition, U.S. forces were once more advancing into their territory. In July 1865, General Patrick E. Connor had sent some 2,000

General Patrick Connor led some 2,000 men to the Powder River region in July 1865. Proclaiming that the Indians north of the Platte "must be hunted like wolves," the general gave his troops license to kill every male Indian over 12 years of age.

soldiers toward the Powder River in search of hostile Sioux. This particular mission did not advance very far. Connor's troops managed to build a garrison 100 miles northwest of Fort Laramie; the post, which came to be known as Fort Reno, later served as an important U.S. cavalry base. But as they pushed farther north, the Sioux continued to elude them. One detachment overshot the Oglala camps and attacked a peaceful group of Arapahos farther west, on the Tongue River. Another traveled too far to the north, marching up and around the Powder River Mountains, only to be chased off by a band of Cheyennes. By the end of summer, the army was plagued by early ice storms. After the soldiers had lost more than 600 of their horses and mules, they retreated south, surviving on horsemeat and burning or abandoning much of their equipment along the way.

Meanwhile, U.S. officials were trying to obtain the Indians' land by other means. By the fall of 1865, a new treaty was circulating at the forts on the Missouri River and at Fort Laramie, and Indian agents were offering gifts to Sioux who would "touch the pen"—make their mark on the paper—and sell access to the Powder River country. Many of the eastern and southern Sioux—Indians who continued to hover around the forts and live on government annuities—were happy to barter away their rights to the Powder River, a region they had not visited in years. Even Spotted Tail, once a staunch ally of the northern Oglalas, agreed to sign the document.

Yet officials realized that until they had signatures from the northern tribes, they would not be able to take the region without a war. They sent runners to the Powder River Sioux, promising goods and asking the Indians to come down and parley. Finally, in May 1866, Young Man Afraid and Red Cloud—who were hoping to bargain for guns and ammunition—rode to Fort Laramie to find out what the whites wanted.

As the talks progressed, so did U.S. preparations for further advancement along the Bozeman Trail. On June 13, 1866, Colonel Henry B. Carrington arrived at Fort Laramie with 700 men in his command. Their assignment—as a Brulé warrior who spoke to Carrington easily discovered—was to build a new road up to the trail and to establish forts along it. Red Cloud quickly got wind of the plan, and discussions came to a halt.

While the Oglala leaders returned to their people, Carrington's army pushed forward. By July, his troops had arrived at Piney Creek, between the Powder and Bighorn rivers at the foot of the Bighorn Mountains, where they proceeded to build Fort Phil Kearny. On August 3, Carrington sent a detachment to the Bighorn River to construct another post, Fort C. F. Smith. Crazy Horse and other warriors, well aware of the impending crisis, followed the soldiers, keeping careful track of their activities and sending reports back to the Oglalas, who were holding their annual Sun Dance on the Tongue River. By the end of the summer, many more Oglala warriors had drifted over to the army's trail and begun attacking the passing travelers at random. From early August to mid-December, they continued their guerrilla campaign, taking the lives of more than 150 whites and nearly stopping traffic along the trail.

All that summer and fall, Red Cloud passed the war pipe through the northern plains, asking Indians from every tribe to join the Oglalas in their effort to drive the whites from the Powder River. By late fall, he had amassed around 3,000 Sioux, Cheyenne, and Arapaho warriors.

Hump, long recognized as an outstanding warrior, was to lead the attack while Crazy Horse directed the decoys. Before they set off for battle, the Indians drilled for days on end, practicing maneuvers with signal flags and mirrors. Signs boded well; a Minneconjou holy man had

The Sioux warrior Pawnee Killer fought beside Crazy Horse at Fort Phil Kearny.

taken a vision-ride, setting out for the woods with a black cloth over his head, and claimed he had caught more enemies than he could hold in both hands.

On December 21, 1866, the Indians struck Fort Phil Kearny. They began by attacking a woodcutting party, whose three-shot distress signal brought Captain William Fetterman, Carrington's main tactical officer, to the rescue. Fetterman had been given clear instructions not to pursue any Indian party, but the decoys hovered so tantalizingly close to the soldiers that they could not resist. Crazy Horse and his small band led the 81 glory-hungry troops farther and farther away from the woodcutters and into the forest. Crazy Horse kept himself moving as shots sliced through the air around him, dismounting to cinch up his pony's war rope, pretending to check its injured hoof, and leading it for a stretch on foot. At a ravine along Peno Creek, miles from the fort, he and his decoys suddenly evaporated over a rise and the full force of Hump's furious warriors plunged down on Fetterman.

Black Elk, then a young boy, remembered the battle: "There were many bullets but there were more arrows— so many that it was like a cloud of grasshoppers all above and around the soldiers; and our people shooting across hit each other." At the end of the fighting, 81 soldiers lay dead; Carrington, in his official report, wrote of mutilations beyond description. Indian losses amounted to only 13 men.

After this startling early victory, Red Cloud's War, as the conflict came to be known, turned into a deadlock.

Indians, trappers, and settlers convene at the Union Pacific Railroad depot at Omaha City, Nebraska, around 1868. The railroad, which ran through the center of southern Sioux territory along the North Platte River, became the target of frequent Indian raids.

The Indians were rebuffed in two later skirmishes at Forts Phil Kearny and C. F. Smith, where they faced the army's repeating rifles. Soon the Indians were limiting their action to guerrilla attacks on supply wagons and terror operations in which they barraged Fort Kearny with arrows. Still, they had accomplished one of their main objectives: the shutdown of the Bozeman Trail.

As it turned out, Indian campaigns elsewhere in the West were working in concert with Red Cloud's offensive to persuade the whites to sue for peace. One of the nation's most cherished projects at the time was the construction of the transcontinental railroad. By the spring of 1866, with the project near completion, Indians traveling back and forth along the North Platte had begun derailing and looting the trains of the Union Pacific Railroad, which

This photograph of prominent Sioux leaders commemorates the 1868 treaty council, at which the Sioux were guaranteed hunting rights to the land between the Black Hills and the Bighorn Mountains. Left to right are Spotted Tail, Roman Nose, Man Afraid of His Horse, Lone Horn, Whistling Elk, Pipe, and Slow Bull.

now ran through that part of the country. With half of the army's 55,000 troops occupying the former Confederate states, many officials believed the United States lacked sufficient forces to defend the railroad from further attacks.

In June 1867, government officials at Fort Laramie produced a new peace treaty, promising lavish gifts to the chiefs who would come and sign it. Though a large number of Sioux leaders—including some from the hostile bands of the north—responded, Red Cloud and the other northern Oglalas told government leaders they would not sign until the forts along the Bozeman Trail were abandoned. After more than a year of negotiations, in a move unprecedented in United States–Indian relations, the government yielded to the Sioux. During the summer of 1868, the weary troops marched out of Forts Reno, Phil Kearny, and C. F. Smith. In November 1868, the grizzled Civil War hero William Tecumseh Sherman, the new commander on the plains, placed before the Indians a document that guaranteed the Sioux hunting rights on all the land between the Black Hills and the Bighorn Mountains "as long as the grass shall grow and the water flow." This same document, as the Indians may not have fully understood at the time, established a reservation in the western half of South Dakota and Nebraska and required the Sioux to set up permanent homes within that region. On November 4, 1868, Red Cloud led a party of 125 Sioux leaders into Fort Laramie, and two days later, one by one, they signed the treaty.

6

BAD BLOOD

An eclipse darkened the skies of the northern plains in the spring of 1870, and Oglala elders saw it as a bad omen. Indeed, signs of trouble were everywhere that year. Barely two years had passed since the signing of Red Cloud's treaty, and already white prospectors were violating it, stealing into the Black Hills and the Powder River region. Meanwhile, the advancing railroad continued to deplete the supply of game along the North Platte. In 1868, in Leavenworth, Kansas, $10 could book passage on a specially chartered buffalo-hunting train, from which a hunter could shoot more than 100 buffalo in a single day. Between 1830 and 1850, the number of buffalo had been blasted down from 75 to 50 million. By the end of the century, this staple of Sioux life would be gone from the northern plains.

In 1869, bowing to the terms of the 1868 treaty, Red Cloud, Man Afraid, and about half of the other northern Oglalas had moved onto an agency—a plot of land surrounding a group of government buildings—on the North Platte River, 32 miles east of Fort Laramie. Spotted Tail and his followers moved to another, on the White River north of the Platte. Crazy Horse, who had refused to sign the treaty and had no intention of complying with it, continued to hunt and raid with other warriors in the

During the 1870s, the northern Oglalas split into two groups: one moved south to the agencies and the other stayed to the north and prepared for war. Young Man Afraid of His Horse, a respected warrior, stood between these factions, moving south but remaining loyal to those who resisted.

"Sportsmen" shoot buffalo from the windows and roofs of a train. By the late 19th century, the number of buffalo on the plains had dwindled drastically.

north. Once again the Oglalas had divided into two factions: one "friendly," the other "hostile." The U.S. government, for its part, had forbidden trade between whites and the Powder River Indians until all the Indians had moved to the reservation. At the same time, officials who hoped to win influence over the tribe alternately courted and intimidated Red Cloud, inviting him to a meeting with the president in Washington, D.C., and taking him on a tour of the East to impress on him the power of the white nation.

Now that Man Afraid had gone to live at the agency, the northern Oglalas at Powder River were without a chief. Crazy Horse, although one of the Oglalas' most respected warriors, was not a great orator, so he was not suited to this position. Still, the Powder River Sioux continued to recognize his commitment and courage, and his influence gradually grew stronger.

In the spring of 1870, Crazy Horse suffered his first profound personal loss: the death of his mentor, Hump. Red Cloud, recently returned from Washington, had come to the Oglala village and was distributing gifts in an effort to bring more Indians to the agency. Perhaps hoping to avoid the leader, whom they now mistrusted, Hump, He Dog, and Crazy Horse took off for a raid against the Shoshones. When their party reached the Wind River, the weather shifted, and sleet began to slap against their faces. They considered turning back; it was the kind of weather that dampened gunpowder, stretched bowstrings, and made horses stumble.

He Dog persuaded them to continue, and they soon charged into the Shoshone camp, where they were quickly overwhelmed. Their horses lost their footing in the slush as they retreated, and soon Hump's horse was injured. When a Shoshone arrow struck Hump in the chest, Crazy Horse could barely see him, so thick was the crowd of enemies around him. Soon Hump was lost in a swarm of angry warriors, and Crazy Horse, beside himself, had to be dragged away as his friend fell to the Shoshones.

A second disaster came that summer. Crazy Horse, still unmarried, had not been able to forget No Water's wife, Black Buffalo Woman. He had begun making regular stops at the Bad Face camp and aroused gossip by talking and walking with his former love, who was by this time the mother of three. Two Bad Face warriors had already called at his father's lodge to warn him of his son's recklessness. Crazy Horse only increased his visits, occasionally bringing gifts; once he came with a collection of elk teeth for Black Buffalo Woman to use in decorating a dress.

One day when No Water returned to his village from a hunting trip, he learned that Black Buffalo Woman had left her three children with another family and ridden off with Crazy Horse for a battle against the Crows. In Sioux culture, a woman could leave her husband for another man as long as her husband was compensated, often by a gift of horses. She could also divorce him on her own, simply by throwing all of his belongings out of the tipi, which was always the wife's property. On the other hand, a husband who caught his wife in adultery had the right not only to divorce her but also to brand her by cutting off her braids or—though this was rare—even her nose.

No Water, according to most accounts, was a jealous and stubborn man, and he approached the insult in his own way. Claiming he was going out hunting, he borrowed a revolver, mounted a mule, and caught up with the war party where they had camped for the night on the Powder River. According to He Dog, Crazy Horse and Black Buffalo Woman were sitting inside a friend's tipi when the flap was thrown open. No Water walked in, pistol first, saying, "My friend, I have come!" Crazy Horse drew his knife to defend himself, but Little Big Man, who was sitting next to him, held his arm back. In that split second, No Water fired point-blank into his rival's face. The bullet entered just below Crazy Horse's left nostril and followed the line of his teeth, fracturing his upper jaw. As the terrified Black Buffalo Woman escaped out the back, No Water fled, grabbing the first horse he saw and blurting out that he had killed Crazy Horse.

Crazy Horse survived, but the wound was slow in healing. It is said that in a delirium he kept mumbling, "Let go of my arm!" Perhaps he had been reminded of his vision. The warriors in his party tried to hunt down No Water but found only his abandoned mule, which they hacked to pieces. The jealous warrior had taken refuge with his brother. Murder was the most serious crime the Sioux knew, and No Water's attack might easily have provoked a war. But long before his jaw had healed, Crazy Horse was using sign language to call for a truce, asking that Black Buffalo Woman be spared reprisals. No Water honored his request and finally sent him three of his best horses as an offering of peace.

The momentary calm was quickly shattered by a third and even harder blow. Barely recuperated from his injury, Crazy Horse received the news that Little Hawk had been gunned down. The young warrior, whose boldness had come to rival even that of his brother, had fallen victim to "big horners"—company miners who liked to keep the Indians hostile so that they could command higher wages for working in a "dangerous" region.

The day after he learned of his brother's death, Crazy Horse, needing to distract himself from his grief, went on a hunting expedition with He Dog and a small party of warriors. The hunters had dismounted and were resting when, suddenly, Crazy Horse saw a warrior jump astride one of their horses and gallop off. He Dog then explained that No Water had stumbled across them, and on seeing Crazy Horse had ridden for his life. "I wish I had known it!" Crazy Horse is said to have replied. "I would certainly have given him a bullet in return for the one he gave me." Then he chased No Water as far as the Yellowstone River. Unnerved, the Bad Face warrior soon retreated to the safety of Red Cloud's reservation, but he would find a way to repay his Hunkpatila rival years later.

Crazy Horse, in the meantime, was in trouble. He had violated his sacred responsibilities as a Shirt Wearer. He had put his own interests before those of the tribe, risked bloodshed, and retaliated after he had accepted an offer of appeasement. The Big Bellies stripped him of his office. He made no protest when the group of 14 armed Bad Faces came for his shirt. Though there was talk among the Bad Faces of giving the position to Red Cloud, no

He Dog, a steadfast friend of Crazy Horse, was said to possess enormous vitality and a keen sense of humor. Historians learned much of what they know about Crazy Horse through interviews with this Oglala warrior.

one took the notion seriously, and the Shirt Wearer tradition slowly died.

Having weathered these adversities, Crazy Horse, now 29 years old, became even more reclusive. Often he would go off alone to hunt and fight, staying away from his camp for days. Black Buffalo Woman, he soon learned, had rejoined No Water and given birth to a light-haired girl, whom many believed was the daughter of Crazy Horse. He Dog was concerned about his friend, and he made a match for him with a 28-year-old Cheyenne woman named Black Shawl. Still despondent over his past, Crazy Horse sent his mother to Black Shawl's camp, warning, "You must say there will be little joy in a life with me." Black Shawl, undaunted, sent back a pair of moccasins beaded with the pattern of the lightning bolt Crazy Horse often painted on his face before battle. They were soon married, and in the fall of 1871, the warrior became the father of a little girl he named They Are Afraid of Her.

By the summer of 1872, Crazy Horse once again had the U.S. Army to contend with. That year an expedition, preparing the way for the Northern Pacific Railroad, set out to survey the land near the Yellowstone River north of the Bighorn Mountains—land that, according to the Treaty of 1868, belonged to the Sioux. U.S. troops accompanied the mission, and eventually, so too would a new commander, a man whose destiny was linked with that of Crazy Horse and, indeed, every Indian on the northern plains: George Armstrong Custer.

A major general and hero of the Civil War, Custer was ambitious, ruthless, and famously lucky in battle. With the end of the war, his rank had dropped to lieutenant colonel, and, determined to advance, he had set out to promote himself the only way he knew how: by fighting the Indians. The southern Cheyennes knew this from bitter experience.

In November 1868, the month the Sioux had negotiated peace with the United States, Custer had led the army's spirited Seventh Cavalry south along the Washita River in Kansas. Sent out to subdue a hostile band of Cheyennes, Custer's regiment had come across Black Kettle's village and, having found an easy target, attacked this band instead. Black Kettle, the same mild, elderly chief whose people had been brutalized at the Sand Creek massacre, died alongside his wife as the two of them rode forward to surrender. Having killed more than 100 Cheyennes, most of them women and children, Custer's

men went on to slaughter the encampment's 800 ponies. Lest anyone returning to the village should survive, they burned the Indians' tipis, clothes, and stores of food. Once again, Custer had ridden to victory.

In August 1873, Custer and a column of 85 men arrived in the heart of northern Sioux territory, leading the way for the 275-wagon survey team. At the time, Crazy Horse and his band were camped at the Rosebud River, near the hunting grounds of the Hunkpapa and No Bow Sioux, Indians renowned for their fierce resistance to white influence. On learning of the troops' approach, Crazy Horse joined forces with Sitting Bull, the brilliant Hunkpapa war leader, and together with a party of Cheyennes they set out to evict the intruders. In the ensuing attacks, both Sitting Bull and Crazy Horse showed enormous daring. According to Sioux accounts, at one point Sitting

General George Armstrong Custer and four Indian scouts pose in front of a Northern Pacific Railroad tent during the Yellowstone River expedition of 1873. Bloody Knife (left), Custer's favorite Crow guide, kneels at the general's side.

Bull walked out into the whites' range of fire to sit and have a smoke. Crazy Horse circled so close to the troops that his horse's tail was clipped with lead. In the end, however, impatience on the part of the Cheyenne warriors, who recognized Custer as their mortal enemy, blunted their efforts. After a set of indecisive skirmishes, Custer chased the Indians off, and the survey party was able to complete its tour by the end of the summer.

That year, Red Cloud's agency was moved away from the Holy Road to a site near the agency of Spotted Tail's Brulés, on the White River just south of the Black Hills. As the cold came on, many more of the Powder River Sioux, attracted by tales of the easy life led at the agencies, drifted south and joined Red Cloud. It was a hard winter for the Oglalas who stayed north. Game was scarce and the Indians often went hungry. Both Black Shawl and They Are Afraid of Her became ill.

In the spring of 1874, Crazy Horse returned from a raiding expedition against the Crows to find that his daughter had died of cholera. Grief-stricken, he took the young girl's body 70 miles west to an open spot in Crow territory, built a scaffold of timber, wrapped her in a red blanket, and laid her to rest. He put some of his daughter's favorite playthings around her to take into the next world: a rattle of antelope hooves, a bladder balloon with pebbles inside, a painted willow hoop, and a deerskin doll. Then he climbed the scaffold, lay down beside her, and mourned for three days.

7

"A GOOD DAY
TO FIGHT"

For as long as the Sioux had known them, the Black
Hills had seemed a place of uncommon power and beauty.
Thickly forested with pine and threaded with crystal lakes
and streams, the hills teemed with game, supported a
wide variety of medicinal plants, and glistened with rocks
and minerals. Sioux legend viewed the hills as a reclining
female figure from whose breasts flowed the fluid of life.
The site of countless Sun Dances, the hills were the sacred
center of the Sioux world.

To the whites, the Black Hills were money. As early
as 1835, prospectors had been probing them, and ulti-
mately the whites would learn that they contained some
of the richest mineral deposits on the continent. In 1858,
a government-sponsored survey party had descended from
the hills bearing rumors of gold. By 1874, with the nation
sunk in a deep postwar depression, talk of the wealth to
be found in the Black Hills had spurred U.S. leaders to
action. That year General Philip Sheridan, who had taken
Sherman's place as commander of the Department of the
Missouri, ignored the Treaty of 1868 and sent Custer at
the head of a 12,000-man expedition to explore the region

and clear the way for a U.S. military post to be established there.

On July 2, 1874, 34-year-old George Armstrong Custer blazed a looping trail west and south from Fort Abraham Lincoln on the Missouri River and across the burning summer plains to the Black Hills, the sacred place the Sioux called *Pa Sapa*. At the edge of the hills, Custer's Santee Sioux scouts refused to venture further into the holy place; Custer and his men continued. Custer was so oblivious to the transgression he was committing that a short time later, when he came upon a small hunting band of Red Cloud's Oglalas, he tried to hire them as guides. The Indians declined.

Custer's explorers reached the hills at the height of their summer splendor. Strawberries, gooseberries, June-berries, huckleberries, and raspberries grew thickly. In his journal, Custer wrote: "In no private or public park have I seen such a profuse display of flowers. Every step of our march that day was amid flowers of the most exquisite color and perfume." By July 27 he had sent an expedition member to the Laramie telegraph office to report his findings: not only rich vegetation but clear water, unlimited lumber, green pasture lands, and "gold among the grassroots." By August 15, 1874, Custer's party was heading for home, the entire crew winding its way down to the plains and back to the Missouri.

Whether Crazy Horse and his band were aware of Custer's brief invasion of the Black Hills is not clear; if so, they were slow to react. The agency Sioux, for their part, did not respond to the incident until the fall, when their outrage nearly escalated to the point of rebellion. On October 22, 1874, J. J. Saville, the government agent at Red Cloud's settlement, had a tall pine cut and brought in from the nearby hills to serve as a flagpole for the agency stockade. Before it could be erected, a band of indignant warriors hacked it to bits, and the alarmed Saville summoned troops from nearby Fort Robinson to quell the disturbance. The incident sparked conflict among the Indians, some of whom felt that the more militant agency Sioux were inviting an army attack. Later that month, Young Man Afraid interrupted a fight; a gang of warriors held Conquering Bear's son, who had taken part in the flagpole riot, pinned to the ground with a bowstring pulled taught across his neck.

That winter, many of the agency Sioux picked up their tipis and traveled north to spend time at the Powder River. For some of these Indians, movement back and forth between the agency and the hunting grounds in the north had become a regular habit. For others, the turmoil at the agency had been too much; they mistrusted the influence of the whites and resented those who were under their spell. These Sioux would add strength to the small band of Powder River loyals who, more and more, looked to Crazy Horse for wisdom and guidance.

In 1875, Red Cloud and Spotted Tail traveled once more to Washington, D.C., hoping to persuade the president to improve reservation conditions. The whites, as the leaders soon learned, had a different goal in mind: they wanted to buy Pa Sapa. By September, a government commission had set up camp between their agencies in order to "treat with the Sioux for the relinquishment of the Black Hills."

Red Cloud, Spotted Tail, and the majority of the agency Sioux, resigned to the loss of their lands, were ready to sell the territory from the start. Selling the Black Hills would mean amending the Treaty of 1868, however, and an amendment required the presence of three-fourths of the tribe's male adults. The Powder River "hostiles," then, would have to be consulted. Young Man Afraid, who was opposed to the sale but hoped it could be avoided

The Hunkpapa warrior Sitting Bull, a great orator and renowned spiritual leader, may have commanded more respect and admiration than any other Sioux patriot. In 1876 he joined forces with Crazy Horse to defend northern Sioux territory from the invading U.S. Army.

peacefully, traveled north to invite his tribesmen to the whites' council. He found nearly 2,000 lodges of Sioux near the Powder River, and a good number of them, lured by the promise of fine food and drink, agreed to go. Further north, Sitting Bull refused. He would never sell the Black Hills, he said, holding a pinch of dust before the council messenger, "not even as much as this." Crazy Horse, remarking dryly that "one does not sell the earth upon which the people walk," sent Little Big Man to keep watch on the proceedings.

On September 20, 1875, the Lone Tree Council began. The government commission sat under a canopy with 120

Fort Robinson cavalrymen filling the space behind them. The attending chiefs assembled in a half-circle, a sea of expectant Sioux, Cheyennes, and Arapahos hovering near. After a minister's blessing and the traditional pretreaty smoke, the commission spokesman announced that they had come to negotiate not only for the Black Hills but also for the Powder River country and the Bighorn Mountains—virtually every inch of nonreservation land that the Sioux possessed.

The chiefs stood for a moment in stunned silence, then walked out of the council. For the next three days they argued over how to respond. Meanwhile, runners had slipped off to inform Crazy Horse and other Powder River leaders of the government's ambitions. As the chiefs worked out their answer, Sioux warriors from the northern camps gathered in the hills above the council site and readied themselves for combat.

The air was tense on September 23, 1875, when the council reconvened. The chiefs had barely reached the council tent when, to the alarm of the government commission, the plains around them exploded with the sound of Indian war whoops. Some 7,000 painted warriors suddenly poured over the ridges, down onto the plain, and through the crowd of onlookers. The mass of warriors circled the tent, chanting war songs. "The Black Hills is my land and I love it," they sang in their native Sioux. "And whoever interferes will hear this gun." They whooped, fired into the air, and jostled the soldiers' horses with their war ponies. When the last of them had ridden in, the warriors drew up all around the whites and brought their ponies to a halt.

Into this ring galloped Little Big Man, stripped to his breechcloth, his face and body painted for war, his chest bloody from the rituals of the Sun Dance. Holding a rifle aloft in one hand and a fistful of cartridges in the other, he screamed, "I will kill the first chief who speaks for selling the Black Hills!" A ghastly silence followed as Indians and whites braced themselves for battle. Finally Young Man Afraid, taking his life in his hands, responded firmly: "Go to your lodges, my foolish young friends. Go to your lodges and do not return until your heads have cooled." Miraculously, they did.

The next round of negotiations took place inside the stockade. After much bartering, Red Cloud agreed to sell the entire Sioux hunting grounds for $6 million and seven generations of annuities. But the other chiefs, each of whom had his own ideas about the worth of the land, could not be persuaded to back him up. The discussions were leading nowhere; after several laborious days, the Lone Tree Council ended without an agreement.

Diplomacy had failed; the government now set in motion a full-scale assault on the Indians. On December 3, 1875, Commissioner of Indian Affairs Edward P. Smith announced that any Indian found off the reservation and in "unceded territory" by January 31, 1876, would be considered hostile and hunted by the army. General Alfred H. Terry assembled the largest force ever to go against the Sioux, a three-pronged command led by Generals John Gibbon, George Crook, and George Armstrong Custer. Custer would move west and south from Fort Abraham Lincoln on the Missouri River. Gibbon, starting at Fort Ellis in central Montana, would move east along the Yellowstone. Crook would start from Fort Fetterman on the North Platte and move north. The Sioux would be caught in the middle.

By February 1876, Crazy Horse knew that soldiers were gathering along the Platte River for a campaign against his people. The Oglalas held a council. Some warriors argued that they could not subject their women and children to an army attack in the dead of winter; they wished to leave for the agency. Referring to his own wife,

General George Crook, one of the army's most active commanders in the late-19th-century Indian wars, sympathized with the Indians and regretted the indignities they suffered under the U.S. government.

Black Shawl, who was sick with tuberculosis, Crazy Horse is said to have told them: "No man can fight when the hearts of his women have fallen down. But for me there is no country that can hold the tracks of the moccasin and the boots of the white man side by side." Still, he continued, he would not pass judgment on those who chose to leave. A few weeks passed, and some of the warriors fled with their families to Red Cloud's reservation. Then Crazy Horse moved his entire camp west to the Chalk Buttes, where they joined Sitting Bull's Hunkpapas.

There was no more talk of surrender. The Oglalas

declared Crazy Horse war chief, and Sitting Bull sent runners to the agencies, calling for all the Sioux to join them in a great encampment at the Rosebud River to celebrate the Sun Dance, hunt buffalo, and fight the whites if necessary. Crazy Horse sent the same message to the northern Cheyennes. By May 1876, more than half of the 10,000 Indians at the Red Cloud and Spotted Tail agencies had headed northwest. The great encampment soon boasted as many as 4,000 warriors.

Crazy Horse did not participate in the festivities but continued to plan for the coming conflict. He wandered alone, perhaps seeking the guidance of his spirit, and from time to time he traveled south to check the position of Crook's forces. After one of these forays, he returned with a brown calfskin to wear as a cape. It was speckled with white like the hailstorm in his vision.

In early June 1876, the massive encampment moved southeast to the valley of the Rosebud River to celebrate the Sun Dance. Attending the dance were huge bands from all the tribes of the northern Sioux: the Oglalas, Hunkpapas, Minneconjous, Brulés, No Bows, and Black- feet; joining them were northern Cheyennes, Assini- boines, Arapahos, and members of two eastern Sioux tribes, the Yanktonais and Santee Sioux. Tales of this Sun Dance, one of the most spectacular in the history of the plains, would be recounted for many years to come.

On June 14, Sitting Bull, as sponsor and leader of the Sun Dance, had 50 small pieces of flesh cut from each of his arms. Streaming blood, he danced around the sacred center pole, staring into the sun for the next 18 hours, until he fell to the ground, unconscious. After reviving him, one of his assistants, Black Moon, relayed Sitting Bull's whispered words to the waiting Indians. He said:

> Sitting Bull wishes to announce that he has just heard a
> voice from above saying, "I give you these because they

Indians gather outside their tipis at a Sioux encampment. In the early summer of 1876, thousands of Sioux and Cheyennes came together at a massive encampment near the Rosebud River to dance, socialize, and prepare for war.

have no ears." He looked up and he saw soldiers and some Indians on horseback coming down like grasshoppers, with their heads down and their hats falling off. They were falling right into our camp.

The Indians were heartened. Surely their fight against the whites would be victorious. Two days later, on June 16, after the camp had moved about 30 miles northwest to graze their ponies on the lush grasses of the Little Bighorn Valley, Cheyenne scouts reported that Crook was on the march from Fort Fetterman. Crazy Horse, stepping into his new role, directed half of the warriors to stay at the Little Bighorn to defend the elderly, the women, and the children. He himself would lead the main war party down to confront Crook.

In less than an hour, about 1,500 Cheyenne and Sioux warriors assembled. When they had danced briefly before the flames of a ceremonial fire, Crazy Horse moved his forces into action. On the morning of June 17, Crazy Horse and his scouts crept over a ridge and looked down into the valley of the Rosebud River. There, far below, were Crook and his 1,200 troops. A little farther up, Crow warriors—hired as scouts by the U.S. Army—were riding up the ridge toward them. Before long, the Crows caught sight of their enemy and stampeded down the slope, screaming, "Sioux! Sioux!" The battle had begun.

It was later said that Crazy Horse had entered the world of his vision before showing his warriors how to fight this battle. Certainly, they fought as they never had before. His forces did not circle their enemy from a safe distance as they had in the past, but swept into the

Sioux warriors attack Crook's cavalry in the Rosebud River valley. This wood engraving was printed in an eastern newspaper in August 1876.

Flamboyant and unorthodox, George Armstrong Custer, or Long Hair, as the Indians called him, was controversial even in his own time. In 1867 he was court-martialed and suspended from the army for a year for abandoning his command without authority.

soldiers' lines again and again. They did not take scalps in this fight—only carbines. They used knives, spears, and clubs to save powder and lead. When the soldiers charged, the Sioux did not respond with the usual heroic rush to meet them, but faded to the side to attack weak points along the army's flanks.

By the end of the conflict, Crook had lost 28 men and fired some 25,000 rounds of ammunition. Drastically short of supplies, he ordered a retreat. The Indians, though they had slightly higher losses—36 men—could count this as a victory. After a brief celebration, Crazy Horse sent warriors down to shadow the fleeing company. Young boys scoured the battlefield for bullet shells, lead, and arrow points. The Indians searched the pockets of the dead and placed the money they found in the hands of warriors from the agency. These men returned to the reservations, bought more powder, and recruited more warriors; the battle of Sitting Bull's vision was yet to come.

Terry, Custer, and the Seventh Cavalry were by this time moving west toward the mouth of the Rosebud River, where Gibbon and his troops had planned to meet them. By the time they arrived, one of Custer's senior officers, Major Marcus Reno, had found Sioux pony trails leading in the direction of the Little Bighorn River. The troops divided once more: Custer's men were to move south along the west bank of the Rosebud River, while Gibbon's column moved in the same direction along the east bank of the Little Bighorn. Terry would bring up the rear, catching the Indians in the middle.

Custer's party soon reached an enormous swath of trampled ground leading south. The trail indicated an Indian force twice the size the whites had expected, and at the sight of it the Crow scouts commenced their death song. Bloody Knife, Custer's Indian assistant, warned him that his troops were about to face more Sioux than they had bullets for. Custer merely told his men, "the largest Indian camp on the North American continent is ahead and I am going to attack it." Then he marched them through the night.

On the morning of June 25, 1876, Custer came in view of the Hunkpapa tipis clustered at the edge of the great encampment and assumed that the clouds of dust rising out of the Little Bighorn Valley were created by Indians stampeding away. Dividing his force into three units, he placed Reno in charge of 130 men and directed him to attack the village while Captain Frederick Benteen slowly followed with about 250 troops and the mule train of extra ammunition. Custer himself would lead a 220-man

The Hunkpapa leader Chief Gall rode beside Crazy Horse in the Battle of the Little Bighorn.

unit up along the bluffs that skirted the valley and attack the Sioux from the opposite side.

The Indians were not stampeding, but waiting. Not long after Reno and his exhausted men opened fire, warriors began streaming in from the north to protect the camp, and it dawned on the whites that they were vastly outnumbered. By the time Crazy Horse came galloping into the fray, a young warrior was able to tell him he had missed the battle. "Sorry to miss this fight," Crazy Horse is said to have shouted, laughing, "but there is a good fight coming over the hill!"

Having caught sight of Custer, Crazy Horse was combing the Hunkpapa camp for more warriors. Before

leaving, he advised the fighting Hunkpapas to save ammunition. "Make them shoot three times as fast," he said. "So their guns will stick and you can knock them down with your clubs." The warriors attacked furiously, and Reno's men were soon fleeing north across the Little Bighorn.

Blowing his eagle-bone whistle, Crazy Horse rallied his men. He took a fresh horse, sprinkled himself with dust, threaded grass spears through his hair like the lightning bolts of his vision, and called out proudly: "It is a good day to fight! It is a good day to die!"

Then, in one coordinated surge, Crazy Horse and a Hunkpapa chief named Gall led their warriors across the

Custer's troops fight the Battle of the Little Bighorn in a drawing by Red Horse, a Minneconjou warrior.

river and up around the bluff above the encampment to meet their enemy. As Custer frantically retreated from Chief Gall's 1,500 warriors, Crazy Horse again and again outflanked him. Finally, boxed in between the river and the bluffs, Custer and his men made for the high-ground, and Crazy Horse and his 1,000 men poured down on top of them.

Here at last the Indians let their bullets fly. Benteen, still far from the battle site, heard fusillades coming so fast they sounded "like the tearing of a great blanket." One warrior, only 14 years old at the time, later recounted:

> I met a soldier on horseback and I let him have it. . . . I kept along beside him, and I took my heavy bow and struck him across the back of the neck. . . . I was mad because I was thinking of the women and little children running down there all scared and out of breath. These Wasichus [whites] wanted it, and they came to get it, and we gave it to them.

In less than an hour, Custer and his 220 troops lay slaughtered. Some 40 Indians were killed in the battle, but the message they had delivered was a strong one. This resounding U.S. defeat, known to the whites as Custer's Last Stand, stunned the entire nation; it would later be known as the turning point in the struggle for possession of the plains.

8

▼ ▼ ▼

THE WEB OF PEACE

Sioux Indians gather for a meeting with government officials at the Red Cloud Agency in 1876. The Sioux are wearing European-style hats in honor of the occasion.

After the Battle of the Little Bighorn, the great encampment broke up, and the Indians dispersed. Many of the agency Indians, though unsure what awaited them there, returned to the reservations. Sitting Bull and his Hunkpapas went back to their hunting grounds in the north, near the lower Yellowstone River, and Crazy Horse led his band, now numbering about 600, northeast toward Bear Butte. The Indians were proud of the blow they had delivered, and those who stayed near the Powder River danced and feasted. Their glory, however, would not last long.

By July 22, 1876, General William Tecumseh Sherman, who was now in control of the reservations, had declared the agency Indians prisoners of war. Pronouncing the Treaty of 1868 invalid on the grounds that the Sioux had prosecuted war, government officials denied the Sioux all rights to their hunting grounds in the northern plains. A new commission drew up a treaty ceding the Black Hills, the Powder River country, and the Bighorn Mountains to the United States. The officials threatened to withdraw the Indians' rations unless they signed it.

Red Cloud and Spotted Tail had little choice; they touched the pen to the treaty. When the leaders learned that they were soon to be moved to a new reservation on the Missouri River, however, Red Cloud balked. Pawnee scouts caught him fleeing the agency, took away his guns and horses, and turned him over to Crook. After this incident, the whites made Spotted Tail head chief of the Sioux, and the deposed Red Cloud was forced to serve time in the Fort Robinson stockade.

Further north, the Sioux who remained outside the agency were being hunted down. Early that fall, General Nelson Miles led a company of troops to the mouth of the Tongue River, built a new post named Fort Keogh, and from there set out after Sitting Bull. By October the Hunkpapa leader, acknowledging the strength of the forces against him, had agreed to meet with the whites in council. Before the talks could progress very far, however, a fight broke out, Miles's troops opened fire on the Indians, and the Hunkpapas escaped to the north. As winter approached, many of them grew weary and turned themselves in. The others followed Sitting Bull and Chief Gall to Canada, where they stayed for the next several years, beyond the grasp of the U.S. Army.

That same fall and winter, Crook led 2,200 troops and 350 Crow and Shoshone scouts in pursuit of Crazy Horse. Before setting out, Crook had gone to the agency and offered a horse and gun to any Indian who would help him track down the Oglala leader. No Water had been one of the first to sign on.

The reckoning began at dawn on November 25, 1876, when Crook struck a Cheyenne village of 150 lodges in a canyon at the head of the Powder River. The troops killed many of the Indians as they slept, shot their ponies, and burned the village, leaving the Cheyennes who escaped to stumble across the frigid country in search of shelter. Three days later, those who survived the cold reached Crazy Horse's camp, by this time situated near the head of the Tongue River.

Crazy Horse could offer them little comfort; both Crook and Miles were on his trail, and the children and the elderly among his followers were suffering terribly. By December, he felt they could endure no more, and he sent eight of his warriors to Fort Keogh to parley with Miles. As the men approached the post carrying a lance tied with a white cloth, a party of Crow scouts charged out and fired on them, killing five of the messengers while the other three fled for safety.

Crazy Horse abandoned the idea of meeting with the whites and struggled valiantly to help his people survive the winter. Members of his band later said that during this time he seemed even more distant than usual, and that he would often wander out into the cold to be alone. Black Elk remembered:

> [Crazy Horse] was always a queer man, but that winter he was queerer than ever. . . . His eyes looked through things and he always seemed to be thinking hard about something. . . . Maybe he was always partway into the world of his vision. . . . Maybe he had seen that he would soon be dead and was thinking how to help us when he would not be with us any more.

On January 1, 1877, Miles's forces discovered Crazy Horse and his band in a canyon near Crazy Woman Creek and mounted a swift attack. The tribe's warriors held the troops off, allowing the other Indians to pack up and escape. For the next week the army pursued them, and the Oglalas were forced to abandon their food and supplies as they floundered through the deep snow. By the time Miles gave up the chase, many of the Indians were frostbitten, and all were weak with hunger.

Finally the whites began delivering messages to Crazy

Horse through the agency Sioux. Lieutenant William H. Clark, the military commander at the Red Cloud agency, sent a party of Indians to the north with an offering of coffee, sugar, and flour and a promise that if Crazy Horse surrendered, the Oglalas would be granted their own agency in the Powder River region. In February, Crook sent another party with a similar message, this time led by Crazy Horse's uncle, Spotted Tail.

Crazy Horse listened to these men, accepted their gifts

General Nelson Miles and his regiment battle Crazy Horse's warriors near Wolf Mountain on January 8, 1877. The Indians lost 16 men in this conflict, their final engagement with the whites.

with gratitude, and sent them back without an answer. Yet as the days wore on and his people continued to weaken, he gradually lost his resolve. By the spring, he had decided they could hold out no longer. As the weather grew warmer, Crazy Horse and his band of Oglala warriors broke camp and headed south for the Sioux agencies.

Red Cloud, leading 100 agency Indians and bearing copious food and gifts from Clark, rode to meet the surrendering Sioux. According to Short Bull, who told the story many years later, Red Cloud approached Crazy Horse some distance north of the agencies and said to him, "All is well; have no fear; come on in." Crazy Horse responded by spreading his blanket for Red Cloud to sit on and offering him his shirt, two Sioux gestures of capitulation.

On May 6, as the Oglalas crossed a plain a few miles away from Fort Robinson, Clark himself rode up to welcome them. The procession paused, and the leaders stopped for a ceremonial meeting. Clark and Red Cloud formed one half of the tiny council circle; Crazy Horse and He Dog sat across from them. Because Crazy Horse had no warbonnet to offer as a token of surrender, He Dog offered his own, along with his shirt, pipe, and tobacco sack. Crazy Horse solemnly extended his left hand to Clark, saying: "Friend, I shake with this hand because my heart is on this side; the right hand does all manner of wickedness; I want this peace to last forever."

Clark answered by offering the Oglalas more food and supplies than they had seen in months. Then, as if to remind his captor of all that was in his power, he advised Crazy Horse, "No matter how fierce or brave a person thinks he is, if he learns to humble himself once in a while, he will be well liked and good things will happen to him."

As the Oglalas continued their march to the fort, thousands of agency Indians gathered to receive them. Crazy Horse, riding together with a cluster of war leaders at the head of the column, could be recognized by his simplicity; he had on a buckskin shirt, wore a single hawk feather in his hair, and had wrapped his braids with strips of otter skin. On either side of him rode his two most trusted allies, He Dog and Little Big Man, while the other warriors, all gloriously painted and dressed for battle, rode in close formation behind them. To the rear trailed the rest of Crazy Horse's loyal followers: altogether more than 800 people and 1,700 ponies, covering a path two miles long.

As the procession entered the White River valley, the surrendering warriors caught sight of the vast crowd of agency Sioux waiting for them at Fort Robinson, and they began to sing. The women and children joined them, and soon the Indians at the agency picked up the song. As the valley filled with voices, even the whites must have sensed the enormous power embodied in the legendary warrior now coming in from battle. One officer observing the scene remarked, "By God, this is a triumphal march, not a surrender."

At Fort Robinson, the Oglalas relinquished their arms and their horses, then set up camp. Soon Crazy Horse began to negotiate with the whites for the promised Powder River reservation. The talks progressed slowly; Clark spoke of sending another Indian delegation to Washington, D.C., so that Crazy Horse and other Sioux leaders could bring their case before the president. The Oglala leader showed little interest in speaking with the "Great White Father."

As Crazy Horse continued to press for the northern territory, he attracted visitors from all around the agency. Younger warriors who had heard tales of his exploits moved their lodges to be near him. Army officers came to see the man who had fought their forces with such courage and tenacity. The whites who met him often remarked on his proud, solemn demeanor. One white visitor later wrote: "The expression of his countenance was one of quiet dignity, but morose, dogged, tenacious and melancholy. He behaved with stolidity, like a man who realized he had to give in to Fate."

For weeks, Crazy Horse resisted Clark's proposal that he meet with the president. The reclusive Sioux warrior had never shown much interest in the business of the whites; he may also have feared a trap. Valentine T. McGillycuddy, the army surgeon who befriended Crazy Horse while treating his wife for tuberculosis, at one point wrote of him: "He was not hunting for any Great Father; his father was with him, and there was no Great Father between him and the Great Spirit." In early July, however, desperate to secure for his people the land they had been promised, Crazy Horse agreed to make the journey. Clark rewarded him by offering to enlist 25 of his people as reservation scouts—a dubious honor, but at least they would have horses and guns. A further promise was made: Crazy Horse and his people would soon be allowed to travel north for a buffalo hunt.

Cautiously, the Oglalas began to look toward the future with renewed hope. Yet while Crazy Horse had been waiting, arguing, and deliberating, doubt and resentment had been mounting among the agency Sioux. With all the attention the Oglala leader was receiving, Red Cloud and Spotted Tail, each of whom had once stood proudly at the center of Sioux-white relations, were growing jealous. If Crazy Horse really did go to Washington, people were saying, he would be made chief over all the Sioux, and both Red Cloud and Spotted Tail would lose their remaining power. No Water, still bent on revenge,

was also using his influence to turn forces against Crazy
Horse. Rumors were soon circulating all over the agencies:
Crazy Horse, word had it, was bitter about captivity and
planned to escape. In separate meetings with Clark and
the local Indian agent, Red Cloud declared that if the
Oglalas were sent north on their buffalo hunt, they would
never return, but would use their guns and ponies to
renew the war. The quiet, brooding warrior, the whites
were informed, could not be trusted.

Agency officials now avoided further talk of the trip
to the north and kept close watch over Crazy Horse. In
August, Frank Grouard, an army interpreter, seemed to
confirm their suspicions. At a council that month, Clark
asked Crazy Horse if he would help the army fight the
Nez Perce, who had entered the northern territory that
had been promised to the Sioux. Crazy Horse resisted for
as long as he could, then responded:

> We are tired of war and talking of war! From back when
> Conquering Bear was still with us we have been lied to and
> fooled by the whites, and here it is the same, but still we
> want to do what is asked of us and if the Great Father
> wants us to fight we will go north and fight until there is
> not a Nez Perce left!

For unknown reasons, Grouard mistranslated the leader's
last words, so it seemed he was promising to fight "until
there is not a white left." Another interpreter corrected
the error, but Clark would not listen. Like lightning, word
spread that Crazy Horse had threatened to fight the
whites.

A few days later, the warrior was dealt the most serious
blow of all. On September 2, Crook, who had heard the
reports about Crazy Horse, returned from his campaigns
in the north and called all of the agency leaders to a
council. As he rode toward the place where the meeting
was to be held, Woman's Dress, now an agency scout,

Woman's Dress, an Oglala whom Crazy Horse had known since childhood, claimed that the celebrated warrior intended to murder General Crook.

stopped him and told him a shattering lie. Crazy Horse, he said, was planning to murder Crook at the council.

The story seemed unlikely, but Crook could take no chances. He summoned the agency chiefs to an emergency conference at the post stockade. Some of the Sioux who came to the meeting insisted that Woman's Dress was right: Crazy Horse was a dangerous man, and it would be best to kill him. Crook was reluctant to go that far, but he agreed that the leader's actions needed to be

contained, and he asked the chiefs to help the army arrest him.

On September 4, eight companies of cavalry and 400 agency warriors, with Red Cloud and other prominent chiefs in the lead, assembled at Fort Robinson to bring in Crazy Horse. When the Oglala warrior caught wind

Ponies and riders crowd toward the corral at the Spotted Tail Agency in 1877. Crazy Horse fled some 50 miles to this post when he learned Crook's men were coming to arrest him.

of the plan, he swept up his family and fled with them to the Spotted Tail agency, some 50 miles away. Clark sent a party of Indians in pursuit and ordered an army detachment to follow; they intercepted Crazy Horse just outside the agency stockade. Army officers, promising the leader he would have a chance to discuss his situation with their commander at the Red Cloud agency, persuaded him to return with them to Fort Robinson.

When they arrived at the fort at dusk the next day, they found thousands of Indians waiting for them. He Dog was among the onlookers, and as the party entered the gates, he approached Crazy Horse with a warning: "Look out—watch your step—you are going into a dangerous place." Little Big Man, who was now an agent of the Indian police, wedged through the crowd to help

Little Big Man, for many years a loyal friend to Crazy Horse, prevented him from fighting his captors at the Red Cloud agency guardhouse. Why Little Big Man restrained his friend has never been clear, but in doing so he fulfilled the final prophecy of Crazy Horse's vision: that his own people would drag him back and defeat him.

guide Crazy Horse toward a small building behind the stockade walls.

No sooner had Crazy Horse been pushed through the guardhouse door than he realized he was being imprisoned. He drew a knife and tried to bolt. A crowd of soldiers rushed in around him, and Little Big Man caught his arms from behind. In the ensuing chaos, Red Cloud could be heard shouting, "Shoot in the middle. Shoot to kill!" While Crazy Horse struggled to break free, a stockade guard lunged forward and thrust the cold steel of a bayonet deep into his body.

At that moment, according to Black Elk, "something went through all the people like a big wind that strikes many trees at once." Crazy Horse, still in the grasp of his captors, dropped to the ground, saying, "Let me go, my friends. You have hurt me enough." He Dog covered him with a blanket; Touch the Clouds brought him to the nearby adjutant's office, and the soldiers sent for McGillycuddy. After a brief examination, the surgeon announced that Crazy Horse, just 36 years old, would not live to see morning.

That night, as the Oglalas gathered quietly around the place where Crazy Horse lay, the warrior's father came and sat beside him. After many hours, Crazy Horse woke for a moment and whispered, "My father, I am badly hurt. Tell the people it is no use to depend on me any more now." Soon afterwards he died.

The next morning, a group of officers placed his body in a coffin and loaded it onto a wagon. Before they could drive off, Touch the Clouds forced them away at gunpoint, then brought the coffin to the camp where the warrior's parents were waiting. According to family legend, until he was buried, every night an eagle would come and walk back and forth on the coffin.

On October 27, 1877, thousands of Sioux Indians, under the guard of U.S. cavalry, began their journey eastward, from the Red Cloud and Spotted Tail agencies to their new reservation on the Missouri River. About 75 miles east of the agencies, there was a sudden commotion, and some 2,000 northern Oglalas broke away from the troops, veered off to the north, and raced for the Canadian border, never to return.

Chronology

FURTHER READING

Ambrose, Stephen E. *Crazy Horse and Custer: The Parallel Lives of Two American Warriors.* New York: Doubleday, 1975.

Brown, Dee. *Bury My Heart at Wounded Knee: An Indian History of the American West.* New York: Holt, Rinehart & Winston, 1971.

Clark, Robert A., ed. *The Killing of Crazy Horse: Three Eyewitness Views by the Indian Chief, He Dog, the Indian-White, William Garnett and the White Doctor, Valentine McGillycuddy.* Lincoln: University of Nebraska Press, 1976.

Connell, Evan S. *Son of the Morning Star: Custer and the Little Bighorn.* San Francisco: North Point Press, 1984.

Erdoes, Richard. *The Sun Dance People: The Plains Indians, Their Past and Present.* New York: Random House, 1972.

Hinman, Eleanor. "Oglala Sources on the Life of Crazy Horse." *Nebraska History* 57, no. 1, (1976).

Kadlecek, Edward, and Mabell Kadlecek. *To Kill an Eagle: Indian Views on the Last Days of Crazy Horse.* Boulder, CO: Johnson Books, 1981.

Neihardt, John G. *Black Elk Speaks.* Lincoln: University of Nebraska Press, 1961.

Olson, James C. *Red Cloud and the Sioux Problem.* Lincoln: University of Nebraska Press, 1965.

Sandoz, Mari. *Crazy Horse: Strange Man of the Oglalas.* New York: Knopf, 1941.

INDEX

118

PICTURE CREDITS

PETER GUTTMACHER, who lives in California, has written extensively for Scholastic Inc., The Children's Television Workshop, and Sundance Publishers. He is also the coauthor of another Chelsea House book, *The Scotch-Irish Americans*.

W. DAVID BAIRD is the Howard A. White Professor of History at Pepperdine University in Malibu, California. He holds a Ph.D. from the University of Oklahoma and was formerly on the faculty of history at the University of Arkansas, Fayetteville, and Oklahoma State University. He has served as president of both the Western History Association, a professional organization, and Phi Alpha Theta, the international honor society for students of history. Dr. Baird is also the author of *The Quapaw Indians: A History of the Downstream People* and *Peter Pitchlynn: Chief of the Choctaws* and the editor of *A Creek Warrior of the Confederacy: The Autobiography of Chief G. W. Grayson*.